Foreword by Marie Diamond

MIND YOUR CONFIDENCE

MIND YOUR BUSINESS

The 7- Step Gateway to Happiness and Success

Karina Klaassen

Disclaimer

This publication contains the opinions and ideas of its author. It is intended to provide helpful and informative material on the subjects addressed in the publication. It is sold with the understanding that the author and publisher are not engaged in rendering medical, health, or any other kind of personal professional services in the book. The reader should consult his or her medical health, or other competent professional before adopting any of the suggestions in this book or drawing inferences from it. The author and publisher specifically disclaim all responsibility for any liability, loss, or risk, personal or otherwise, that is incurred consequently, directly or indirectly of the use and application of any of the contents of this book. Some names and identifying characteristics have been changed.

Contents

To my daughter,

Even before you were born, we decided to raise you with confidence. You are the embodiment of self-assurance. Your journey has been a constant source of inspiration, teaching me the true essence of believing in oneself. You excel at setting boundaries and know exactly what you want and how you want it, all with unwavering confidence. We have done everything in our power to nurture and support your self-belief. You are living proof, and my inspiration, of how confidence and self-love can be cultivated. This book is dedicated to you, as a testament to your strength and as a guide for others to find their own path to self-confidence.

With all my love,
Karina Klaassen

Foreword

As a master of Feng Shui and the power of energy alignment, I have long understood the profound impact our inner worlds have on shaping our outer realities. When I first encountered "Mind Your Confidence, Mind Your Business," I was immediately drawn to its harmonious blend of heartfelt narrative and practical guidance – a perfect symphony of personal growth and professional success. As Master Teacher of the Law of Attraction, I emphasized in the global phenomena The Secret, the importance of harnessing the energy around us to manifest our deepest desires. This book takes that principle a step further, guiding readers on an inward journey of self-discovery, transforming insecurity into self-love, and ultimately, greater prosperity in business and life. With its powerful toolkit of personal anecdotes, scientific insights, and transformative exercises, this book equips you with the tools to cultivate an unwavering belief in your abilities.

What truly resonated with me was the author's authenticity. By courageously sharing her vulnerabilities and triumphs, she creates a profoundly relatable and inspiring narrative. This vulnerability not only engages but also empowers readers to confront their own challenges with resilience and emerge stronger. The exercises offer step-by-step methods to boost confidence and apply it across all aspects of life, including the professional sphere. But what sets this book apart is its holistic approach. It doesn't merely focus on building self-confidence for personal gain but emphasizes the importance of this self-assuredness in contributing to a harmonious and successful work environment. This perspective aligns seamlessly with the principles of Feng Shui, where balance and positive energy flow are key to achieving true prosperity and happiness.

I am confident that "Mind Your Confidence Mind Your Business" will be a transformative guide for many. It is a profound reminder that our inner worlds shape our outer realities. By cultivating self-love and confidence, we not only enhance our personal well-being but also create a ripple effect that positively impacts our professional lives and the lives of those around us. Embrace the journey this book offers and allow it to guide you towards a more confident, harmonious, and prosperous life.

With love and light,

Marie Diamond

Feng Shui Master, Star in The Secret

Executive Producer and Star of TV Show Feng Shui your Life

6 times Global Best seller Author

www.MarieDiamond.com

Introduction

Have you ever seen a person with low self-esteem being happy? Well, I haven't! Being insecure influences so many aspects of our lives that if you want to change ONE thing in your life, gaining confidence is the one that will help you move forward.

I am speaking from experience; I began in a position of having very low self-esteem and learned to love myself unconditionally. The possession of confidence has totally changed my life for the better, and I feel much happier in almost every area of my life. As a result, I'm able to be more honest in my relationships and I can now handle difficult situations much more easily. I went from not wanting to lead a team at work to loving it and to being a successful entrepreneur.

Self-love helps you to be a better leader and a better human being for others and yourself. The fact that you are reading this book implies that you can use more confidence in your life and work too. Congratulations on your first step to realizing that you can gain more confidence.

- Do you want to know how it feels to be happy?

- Do you believe it is impossible to be confident?

- Do you believe you cannot love yourself?

Great news: when you consciously do the exercises in this book, you will be happier and more successful. My experience working with many clients and teams proves that confidence, self-love, and happiness can be cultivated, resulting in success.

It is my wish for you to feel that you have everything inside you to be more confident and eventually unconditionally love yourself.

Let self-confidence WORK for you, not against you.

Karina Klaassen

CHAPTER 1

What Is Self-Confidence?

I remember being six years old, lying under the bed with my heart pounding hard. My parents just bought a reproduction of a famous painting, and the varnish was still a bit wet, so my father told me not to touch it. And what did I do? I touched it. Knowing my father, I also knew that punishment would follow, so I ran as quickly as I could and hid under the bed. It was only a matter of seconds before he found me, grabbed my leg, and hit me. Right there at that moment, I decided not to be naughty again as I was so afraid of my father's anger.

At that instant, I decided to be a 'good' girl all the time. I spent the next few years trying to stay under the radar, and as a result I became a shy and insecure child. I was afraid to speak up, let alone go against my father. Times were different then; I know my parents loved my sister and me and raised us the best they could. My mum was an insecure woman. She was so pretty, yet always seemed to doubt herself. She was very concerned about our well-being and overprotective. We always had to be 'careful' when doing something, an attitude which did not contribute to cultivating self-confidence. However, there was one area she excelled in, and still does—loving me and my sister unconditionally.

I grew up a self-conscious child. I had short hair, and on top of that, I needed glasses at a young age. The children at school made many jokes about my glasses and often called me 'boy', which led me to rebel against the nickname by styling myself in a distinct way with skirts and dresses. Despite being insecure and wanting to be invisible in many areas, fashion was one area where I was confident; I always had my own style, loved wearing colourful clothes and experimenting with different designs. Funnily enough, there were no jokes about the way I dressed. Looking back, I believe this was because I wore my clothes with confidence. Even today, I receive many compliments about my style.

Growing up as an insecure child had a profound impact on my early professional life. When I first entered the workforce as an assistant in a small company, I carried those insecurities with me, often doubting my abilities and shying away from challenges. However, through a journey of personal development, inner reflection, and transformative experiences, I gradually built the self-confidence that has been instrumental in my success as a businesswoman. Today, I am passionate about sharing the lessons I've learned to help others cultivate the self-confidence they need to thrive in their careers and personal lives.

Confidence is not simply a reflection of past successes; it also plays a vital role in shaping future outcomes. Research has shown that "individuals with higher levels of self-confidence are more likely to set challenging goals, persist in the face of obstacles, and ultimately achieve better results." (Bouffard-Bouchard, 1990).

In the following chapters, we will delve deeper into the concept of self-confidence and explore practical strategies for building and maintaining it in the workplace. Through a series of exercises and insights drawn from my own experiences and the experiences of others, you will learn how to:

- Identify and overcome self-limiting beliefs

- Set healthy boundaries

- Cultivate self-compassion and resilience

- Harness the power of self-love to fuel your personal and professional growth.

By the end of this book, you will have the tools and knowledge you need to transform your self-confidence and unlock your full potential in your career and beyond.

We'll begin by determining what self-confidence is. One of the most common descriptions of self-confidence is the belief in one's own abilities, skills, and judgment. It's often characterized by a sense of assurance and trust in oneself to handle various situations and challenges effectively. Self-confidence can manifest in behaviours such as assertiveness, resilience in the face of setbacks, and a willingness to take risks. It's essentially about having a positive perception of oneself and one's capabilities.

There are various words associated with self-confidence:

self-assurance

self-esteem

self-regard

self-respect

self-worth

When we look at different areas in our life, there may be areas where we are showing confidence and other areas where we are not. For example, you may be very good at your job and have confidence in how you do it; however, if you must give a presentation to a group of people, you may feel insecure about your ability to speak publicly.

There's an old folklore tale about a person visited by both a devil and an angel, each sitting on a shoulder, offering conflicting advice. I call these my 'puppets'. They talk to me - one may be supportive, while the other may undermine my confidence. Shirzad Chamine, who developed Positive Intelligence, categorizes these 'puppets' as "Saboteurs" and "Sages."

Saboteurs are those nagging voices in your head that plant doubt or disrupt your progress. They manifest as the ever-critical Judge, the perfection-seeking Controller, or the self-pitying Victim. These puppets, driven by fear, hinder you from reaching your full potential.

In contrast, Sages act as your inner wise guides. They provide clarity, enhance empathy, and encourage smart action. These are the puppets that uplift and support you.

The key is to recognize Saboteurs when they surface and prevent them from taking control. Instead, aim to engage your Sage more frequently. This increases your mental resilience, enhances creativity, and improves your overall well-being, both personally and professionally. Research indicates that women tend to start experiencing self-criticism at a younger age than men. We all have these internal voices. What kind of voices speak to you? Are you aware of what they're saying?

How does it show you lack confidence?

Some of our behaviours may not even be recognized as a result of low self-esteem, as it can disguise itself in many ways, such as:

- Negative social comparisons

- Trouble asking for help

- Worry and doubt

- Difficulty accepting compliments

- Negative self-talk

- Fear of failure

- Poor outlook on the future

- Lack of boundaries

- Being a people-pleaser

How many boxes do you tick?

In either case, a lack of personal worth and value can have a negative impact on life and wellness.

Why do we need self-confidence?

I am convinced that confidence influences almost everything we do. Though it may vary from person to person, even for simple actions such as going outside or showing up to a birthday party, confidence is needed.

Here are some examples of how insecurity can affect our lives:

Relationships

Low self-esteem can affect our ability to form and maintain healthy relationships and set boundaries. It may lead to feelings of inadequacy, fear of rejection, and difficulty in trusting others, which can strain friendships, romantic relationships, and familial bonds.

In my first real relationship, I was very insecure, and we did not bring out the best in each other. My ex used to say that my legs were fat, which made me feel awful. My self-esteem was so low that I completely believed what he was saying. If I had the self-love I have now, I would not have allowed his remarks to make me doubt myself.

When you are at work and do not feel confident, you probably will not take any risks and stick to what you know. In addition, you probably will not raise your hand to volunteer when asked to do something new. And you may miss out on great opportunities, potentially even being passed over for a promotion.

MENTAL HEALTH

Persistent low self-esteem is often linked to mental health issues such as depression, anxiety, and stress. Negative self-perceptions can worsen these conditions and make it challenging to seek help or engage in self-care practices.

In my thirties, I suffered from a burnout. I was a working mum, and my mother was diagnosed with cancer. I wanted to be there for my mother during her chemo treatments, be a good mum, look good, be a good housewife, and an amazing employee. In short, I wanted to be a steady rock for everyone and please them. After a while, I began to suffer from pains in my joints, which I blamed on being busy, not sleeping well, etc. Apparently, I did not listen very well to my body and as a result, I could barely sleep because of the pain. But I thought that with enough willpower, I could overcome this body that was not listening to my mind.

Until one moment, I wanted to get up in the morning and could barely walk anymore. Eventually, I was sent to a rehabilitation centre for people with chronic pain. I believed I was way 'too healthy' to be there and felt ashamed for taking up someone else's place there. However, soon I realized I was quite far from being healthy. Acknowledging that was the first step to my recovery.

Do you recognise that thinking enough willpower will help?

Physical Health

Research suggests that low self-esteem can contribute to poor physical health outcomes; individuals with low self-esteem may be less likely to prioritize their physical well-being, leading to unhealthy lifestyle habits such as poor nutrition, lack of exercise, and substance abuse.

One of my clients battles with low self-esteem and pushes herself hard to demonstrate her competence at work. However, in the process, she neglects self-care, claiming she lacks time for exercise, often skips meals, and doesn't take breaks. Eventually, she became utterly exhausted and had to take time off to recharge her batteries. All too often, we prioritize others over ourselves. Ensure adequate rest, nutrition, and relaxation to function optimally. Do you love yourself enough to take care of your own mental and physical health like it was that of a loved one?

Decision Making

Low self-esteem can undermine our confidence in decision-making, which may lead to indecision or reliance on other people for validation. In doing so, you may be limiting your personal growth and autonomy, as well as limiting opportunities for self-improvement and achievement. Additionally, low self-confidence may lead to self-doubt. If you doubt yourself, how can you trust your own good judgement? Years ago, I saw an advertisement for an amazing job, but I didn't meet all the requirements and started doubting myself: "Can I do this? Should I apply? Or maybe not?" By the time I was finally ready to apply, the vacancy was already filled. Unfortunately, it's a common issue, especially for women, who often feel they need to tick all the boxes before applying for a job, while men tend to apply even if they don't have all the required skills. How does your confidence affect your decision-making?

There is a link between self-care and decision-making. Taking care of our physical and mental health can boost our confidence and improve our emotional state, making us more likely to take positive actions and make better decisions. When we neglect self-care, our stress and self-doubt can overshadow our potential, leading to missed opportunities.

Life Satisfaction

How do you feel when you are insecure? Happy? All the people I have coached over the years feel miserable when they are lacking self-confidence. Feelings of worthlessness or self-doubt may overshadow achievements and positive experiences, leading to a diminished sense of joy and purpose in life. In our pursuit of happiness, have a look at how confident you are and work on cultivating more self-love. Often people look outside of themselves to feel worthy, e.g., by being dependent on others or buying lots of unnecessary material possessions and using social media excessively.

Goal Pursuit

When you have low self-esteem, you may set lower aspirations as you believe you cannot achieve them. When I left my managerial job, I asked one of my co-workers if she wanted to apply for the position, but she didn't have enough confidence and decided not to. I strongly believed she could do the job. How often are you underselling yourself or avoiding pursuing your goals altogether due to fear of failure or feelings of unworthiness?

Why Do You Need Self-Confidence at Work?

You may assume that having less confidence does not impact your work, but reality shows that is not the case.

When I was working for a big multinational company, I was part of a technical team. I was asked to organize an event for the entire team, which made me feel honoured. I rented a beautiful sailing boat for a trip with the whole team. I meticulously planned everything and made sure there was enough to eat and drink, etc. On the day of the event, I arrived early at the harbour where the boat was docked to ensure that all was perfect. One by one, the other team members came to the event, and eventually, my line-manager arrived. Once everybody was settled on the boat and we were about to sail away, my manager walked up to me, thanked me for all the work I had done, said goodbye, and wished me a good trip back home. In other words: I was only the organizer and not allowed to join the team. I felt awful and so small, as if I was not good enough. I went to my car and cried. I truly felt humiliated. In all fairness: he had never mentioned that I was joining the event; it was something that had gone unsaid as I was part of that team. If I look back now, I would have had a private conversation with him in which I would have expressed my desire to join the team—of which I was a part—and would not have let myself be sent home. However, because I was so insecure at the time, I provided the opportunity for him to send me home. This was a great learning experience for me: be clear about your expectations, communicate them clearly, and stand up for yourself.

This is just a small example of how insecurity can impact our work and lives. Below, we will explore more areas that demonstrate how confidence impacts our work.

PERFORMANCE

Numerous studies have found a positive relation between self-confidence and job performance. Employees with higher levels of self-confidence tend to perform better in their roles, take on challenges more readily, and persist in the face of setbacks. Confident entrepreneurs are more successful because they take calculated risks, view their actions positively, and are less swayed by failure.

When I was working for a consultancy firm as the team lead in a big project, a consultant called Joe was added to the team. Unfortunately, his reputation was not very good, and I was informed that his performance was mediocre. In all honesty, I found myself not looking forward to having him on the team. However, when I got to know Joe, I discovered that during a previous assignment, his confidence had become very low, which had resulted in some conflict and low performance. We agreed that I would coach him, and by practicing positive self-talk and setting small, achievable goals, Joe gradually built his confidence up. Within a few months, he was thriving. His confidence grew, he felt much more at ease, and his performance had become excellent. Nowadays, he is a successful manager of his own team.

LEADERSHIP EFFECTIVENESS

Self-confidence is important for effective leadership, particularly self-leadership. Leaders who exhibit self-confidence are more likely to inspire trust and respect among their team members. They will communicate their vision effectively and will make decisions with conviction. I believe that to be a good leader, you need a good dose of confidence and self-knowledge. First, you need to know how to lead yourself, and only then can you lead others. In my first managerial job, I barely knew myself and felt like I had to prove myself. Fortunately, as my confidence grew, I became a more effective (and relaxed) leader, which was beneficial for everyone.

Have you ever felt like you needed to prove yourself in a new role? How did your confidence impact your effectiveness as a leader and your ability to lead yourself?

CAREER OPPORTUNITIES

Research suggests that people with higher self-confidence are more likely to pursue career advancement opportunities, such as seeking promotions or taking on leadership roles. Their belief in their abilities enables them to pursue their goals with determination. They tend to 'go for it,' whereas when you doubt yourself, you may not even apply as you believe you are not capable.

My father always told me: 'Kings, emperors, and admirals: they all have to go to the bathroom." I thank him for teaching me that. And even though I sometimes let myself be overpowered because of someone's rank, I realize that in the end, we are all humans and all equal. Maybe some of my power comes from that realization.

RESILIENCE

Self-confidence serves as a buffer against stress and adversity. People who possess confidence in their abilities are better equipped to handle challenges, setbacks, and criticism, bouncing back more quickly and maintaining their performance levels. The effect this has, is huge. We will dig into this idea more in Chapter 6.

JOB SATISFACTION

"A meta-analysis of core self-evaluations traits, including self-esteem and generalized self-efficacy, found that these traits are strongly correlated with job satisfaction" (Judge & Bono, 2001). Employees who feel confident in their skills and abilities tend to experience more satisfaction with their work, leading to higher levels of engagement and motivation.

Imagine that you have been asked to give a presentation on a subject you know nothing about. Would you feel confident about doing so? On the other hand, if you know a lot about a subject, like how to use Instagram, it will be much easier for you to give a presentation about it. This doesn't mean you won't feel a little nervous about presenting, but at least you know the subject, and that can boost your confidence.

TEAM COLLABORATION

Employees with self-confidence are more likely to actively contribute to team projects, share their ideas and opinions, and collaborate effectively with colleagues. They are more inclined to raise their hand when asked to contribute. On the other hand, individuals with low self-esteem may tend to shy away from such opportunities.

When one of my clients announced that a foreign division of the department would be closed and people would be laid off there, several people in the team became nervous. Would they have to take on additional and new tasks they were not skilled in? On the other hand, the more confident employees in the team saw this as a great opportunity to expand their knowledge and maybe learn new skills. Do you see how being confident influences the team and how they work together?

CUSTOMER INTERACTIONS

When you want you to buy a computer: would you rather be served by someone who is very insecure and hesitant or someone who seems confident and expresses knowledge? Can they convince you? Or if you must have surgery and your surgeon seems insecure: do you feel you can trust that person to do the surgery?

Confident employees are more likely to convey competence, trustworthiness, and professionalism, enhancing customer satisfaction and loyalty.

Exercise: Focus on Goals

What are your dreams? Do you want to be promoted or have a higher salary? Would you like to feel more at ease at work, or feel less stress?

Look at your goal and let that be the biggest motivator for you to gain more confidence. Write down your goals (and write them in present tense, as if you have already achieved them) and keep the focus. Whenever you feel you go off track, look at your goals and focus on the outcome you want to achieve. Keep your eye on the 'prize' constantly. It's important to FEEL the outcome. Once you achieve your goals, how will your life look and how and who will you be? By doing the exercises in this book, your confidence will grow.

How Would You Rate Your Confidence?

Before we dig into how to boost your confidence, let us establish a baseline. Where are you now? This way, you can monitor the progress you are making over time. Of course, we would all love to make things happen overnight, but gaining more confidence and cultivating self-love is a process, so allow yourself plenty of time to improve. When you plant a seed, it does not immediately sprout roots. A seed requires conditions to grow; good soil, fresh water, lots of sunlight, and time. Remember that confidence is also a seed and can't be expected to grow overnight.

Exercise: Survey

Please choose one of the answers for each of the following questions and write down your choice:

1. How confident are you about your physical appearance?
A) Not very confident
B) Moderately confident
C) Very confident

2. How confident do you feel about your abilities to handle challenges at work or in your career?

A) Not very confident

B) Moderately confident

C) Very confident

3. How confident are you in your communication skills, including speaking, listening, and expressing yourself effectively?

A) Not very confident

B) Moderately confident

C) Very confident

4. When it comes to personal relationships, how confident are you in forming and maintaining meaningful connections with others?

A) Not very confident

B) Moderately confident

C) Very confident

5. How confident are you in managing your finances and making sound financial decisions?

A) Not very confident

B) Moderately confident

C) Very confident

6. Regarding your physical health and fitness, how confident are you in your ability to maintain a healthy lifestyle and make positive choices?

A) Not very confident

B) Moderately confident

C) Very confident

7. When faced with adversity or setbacks, how confident are you in your resilience and ability to bounce back?

A) Not very confident

B) Moderately confident

C) Very confident

8. How confident do you feel about setting and achieving personal goals or aspirations?

A) Not very confident

B) Moderately confident

C) Very confident

9. In social situations or group settings, how confident are you in your ability to contribute meaningfully and feel comfortable?

A) Not very confident

B) Moderately confident

C) Very confident

10. When it comes to decision-making, how confident are you in your ability to trust your instincts and make choices that align with your values?

A) Not very confident

B) Moderately confident

C) Very confident

Scoring:

For each answer, assign the following points:

A) 1 point

B) 2 points

C) 3 points

Add up the points from all 10 questions to determine your overall confidence score. The higher the score, the greater the self-perceived confidence in various areas of life.

11 points (Low Confidence): It seems that there are various areas where you have room to grow. The good thing is that when you work on one area to gain more confidence, you will find that in other areas, you automatically gain more confidence too. You are on the right track with this book. Every step forward, no matter how small, is a step towards personal empowerment.

12-21 points (Moderate Confidence): In various aspects of your life, you already possess a solid foundation of confidence. This score indicates that you're already on the path to self-assurance. Look at the areas in your life where you want to gain more confidence and work on those. With each challenge you face and overcome, you'll continue to strengthen your belief in yourself.

22-33 points (High Confidence): Your high confidence score shows a deep sense of self-assurance and resilience. You approach life's opportunities and challenges with unwavering belief in your abilities. Your confidence inspires others and opens doors to limitless possibilities. However, even with high confidence, there's always room for growth and refinement. Embrace each new experience as an opportunity to further strengthen and expand your confidence, empowering yourself to reach even greater heights.

No matter what your scores are, life will always throw some challenges your way that may cause moments in which you feel low self-esteem. The trick is how to bounce back and regain your confidence.

"Life isn't about waiting for the storm to pass; it's about learning to dance in the rain."

CHAPTER 2

What Is Causing Low Self-Esteem?

Some people innately have more confidence than others. Maybe you started out with a lot of confidence but, due to circumstances, it has vanished; on the other hand, maybe you always struggled with confidence issues. In this chapter, we'll explore some of the reasons which might contribute to low self-esteem in both children and adults.

Early Experiences

Childhood experiences can profoundly shape confidence and self-esteem. Below are some examples of how different aspects of early experiences can impact confidence.

Parental Attachment

According to John Bowlby's attachment theory, children who form secure attachments with their caregivers are more likely to develop higher self-esteem and confidence as they grow older (Bowlby, J. (1969). Attachment and Loss: Vol. 1. Attachment. New York: Basic Books). This foundational attachment helps them trust others and themselves. When children feel safe and secure, they're more confident exploring the world around them. They bounce back from challenges and setbacks way much more easily because they know their parents will support them no matter what. Having that rock-solid foundation helps build resilience and self-confidence that sticks with them as they get older.

When I was pregnant with our daughter, my husband and I sat down to discuss what kind of childhood we wanted our baby to experience. We reflected on our own upbringings and the struggles we faced, particularly with self-confidence. That's when we decided that fostering confidence and self-assurance would be a major focus in how we raise our child. We set the intention to be ever-present and supportive parents who nurture our child's belief in themselves from the very beginning.

With this approach of building confidence through consistent support, we saw our daughter grow up and navigates life's many challenges while staying true to herself. Our aim for confident parenting definitely paid off.

Parenting Style

Authoritative parenting, which combines warmth and support with clear boundaries and expectations, fosters a healthy balance of autonomy and responsibility in children. They feel valued and respected, leading to greater confidence in their abilities to navigate challenges and make independent decisions.

A friend of mine once said that children need "loving boundaries instead of boundless love." As a parent, I found one of the most difficult things to do was to set boundaries and stick to them. However, the benefit of doing so is that children know what to expect and that they can trust you. Every now and then, they will try to push these boundaries; that is healthy and normal. The important thing is that they know what the boundaries are and that you as a parent are clear about your authority. Parenting in this way gave our daughter trust and also a framework she could rely on.

Positive Reinforcement

MISUNDRESTANDING

What is the first thing you notice when reading the word above? Do you notice the E is misplaced? We are so conditioned to see what is wrong that we might not notice that out of these 12 letters, 11 are placed correctly. Is that how we look at ourselves as well?

We are raised to focus mainly on faults and flaws rather than achievements and virtues, which leads to binary thinking: it is either good or bad, right or wrong. When a child comes home from school with a report card, we are conditioned to look at the lower scores first. Let us make a habit to mention both; praise the good marks before you ask about the lower scores. Most importantly, show your child that even though they have been awarded a lower score, they are still great kids and that you love them. Even when you have a tough discussion with them about school, you must praise them for the effort they put in—if they did— and show them unconditional love that is not dependent on their grades at school. Praising a child for their creativity or perseverance in completing a task builds their confidence and motivation to tackle new challenges. This requires a careful balance. Praising a child for everything they do seems like a great idea to boost their confidence, but in the light of adversity, in the long term, they will not learn how to deal with constructive criticism, which is also a problem.

Role Modelling

Parents serve as primary role models for their children, and parents' behaviours and attitudes greatly influence how children perceive themselves and others. For instance, a child who observes their parent demonstrating confidence, assertiveness, and problem-solving skills is more likely to internalize these qualities and exhibit similar behaviours.

I am not a perfect parent and have made many mistakes. Nevertheless, my husband and I showed our daughter that when things go wrong, we pick up the pieces and continue, we persevere even when things are difficult, and try to maintain a positive and growth mindset.

Peer Interactions

Positive peer interactions, such as forming friendships and engaging in cooperative play, contribute to children's social development and confidence. Feeling accepted and included by others boosts self-esteem and provides opportunities for learning and growth in social skills. During our lives, we sometimes have the privilege to have relationships with people that unconditionally love us. They believe in us and make us understand that we are good enough, despite our flaws. They can tell us the truth and yet love us wholly. Let us nurture those relationships as they are the mirrors of our True Self.

EARLY EDUCATIONAL EXPERIENCES

Early educational environments that prioritize individualized learning, encourage curiosity, and provide opportunities for success can enhance children's confidence and motivation to learn. For instance, a preschool classroom that celebrates each child's unique strengths and interests fosters a positive sense of self and a love for learning.

These examples illustrate how early experiences within the family, social, and educational contexts shape children's confidence and self-esteem. Positive and nurturing experiences lay the foundation for healthy development, resilience, and life-long confidence.

In practice, there are no perfect families; there are always situations that have an influence on our self-esteem, even if not meant to be. Sometimes a simple remark can 'scar' you for life.

A client of mine confessed that when she had her first job at 15, her 26-year-old manager told her she was only 'book' smart but was not really intelligent. This passing remark influenced her life and self-esteem greatly. Why would you give anyone the privilege to lower your confidence? And do you believe everything they say? In this case, I'd add that it is not realistic to expect working experience from a 15-year-old.

When I studied design in London during my first year in college, one of the teachers told me: "Karina, you cannot draw." For the next two years, every time I had to create a drawing, it took me hours and hours; the moment my pencil reached the paper, I heard his negative words in my mind. During year three, I had a teacher who said he would teach me how to draw and when I graduated with first class honours, the same teacher from year 1 admitted that, 'Karina can actually draw well." The morale of this story is that we can mistakenly assign our own power to words that someone once said to us, and as a result, we create stories in our heads and start believing them as if they are true.

SOCIAL COMPARISON

Children and adults often engage in social comparison, where they evaluate themselves in relation to others. Constant comparison to *perceived* standards of success or attractiveness can lead to feelings of inadequacy and low self-esteem. Social media is an example of this, because I hear so many clients talk about the effect that seeing successful people has on them. On one hand, this can be a motivation, but on the other hand, the result of so much comparison is a net negative. People ask themselves unhelpful questions like: do I look the same? Does my life look anything like that? The truth is that many pictures and successful stories are just that — "stories"— and most of them are not real or true. Filters and careful lighting greatly enhance existing beauty, and flaws can be easily airbrushed out, etc.

Negative Feedback

Criticism and negative feedback, whether from parents, teachers, peers, or other authority figures, can undermine confidence and reinforce self-doubt. Harsh or overly critical feedback without constructive support can be particularly damaging.

At work, during the annual appraisal conversations, line managers often start the conversation telling you what you did well. After that praise, they start talking about what did not go well and how this needs to be changed. Here is emphasis on the areas where we need to 'grow'. However, depending on the kind of job, not all skills are as important and when you are competent for the job, I firmly believe that it is important to focus on developing our strengths even further.

Think about Ronaldo, one of the best soccer players ever. He's amazing at scoring goals. But what if someone told him to be a keeper instead? He might get a bit better at it, but he'd never be as good as he is at scoring. It's the same with us at work. When we struggle to improve skills, we lack naturally or dislike, our progress is often limited despite significant effort. But it takes a lot of energy and we'll probably never be great at it.

Instead, if we focus on what we're already good at, like Ronaldo sticking to scoring goals, we can become excellent. This helps us feel more confident and do much better in our jobs.

However, this doesn't mean we should never try to improve our weaker areas, especially if they're crucial for our roles. The key is to approach these improvements strategically. For instance, I used to lack confidence in public speaking, which was essential for my job as a line manager in multinational companies. Instead of avoiding it, I identified why I struggled and focused on learning techniques from skilled presenters. By addressing this specific weakness that was holding me back, I transformed it into a strength. Nowadays, I love speaking in public.

The lesson here is to be selective about which weaknesses to address. Focus primarily on your strengths, but don't shy away from improving skills that are truly critical for your success. This balanced approach can lead to both professional growth and increased confidence.

Physical Appearance

Physical appearance can play a big role in how confident someone feels, as society often places significant emphasis on external appearance. People who feel dissatisfied with their physical appearance may experience lower self-esteem and confidence, particularly in environments where appearance is valued or scrutinized, such as in certain workplaces or social settings.

While feeling good about one's physical appearance can certainly contribute to confidence, it's not the only or most important thing that matters. Some individuals may feel confident regardless of their physical appearance, while others may struggle with confidence despite meeting societal beauty standards. I bet that even the most beautiful woman in the world thinks she has several imperfections she is not confident about.

There is a lot of emphasis on how and what people should look like. If you look different or have disabilities, this may impact your self-confidence a lot. And on purpose, I wrote down MAY impact, as there are also plenty of examples of people with disabilities who are very confident and have learned to love their appearance.

Always remember: 'beauty is in the eye of the beholder'.

Traumatic Experiences

As my own story clearly shows, traumatic events such as abuse, neglect, or significant life disruptions can profoundly impact self-confidence. These experiences may create feelings of fear, insecurity, and a lack of trust in oneself and others.

Personality Traits

Our personality is made up of different traits, and some of these traits can affect how confident we feel. For example:

- Perfectionism: People with this trait always want things to be just right. They might worry a lot about making mistakes, which can make them scared to try new things.

- Introversion: This is a trait where people prefer quiet, alone time. They might find it hard to speak up or share ideas in group settings.

These are just two examples of personality traits. While they're part of who we are, they don't define our entire personality. However, traits like these can make it harder for people to feel confident in certain situations. Personality is complex and includes many traits. Having one trait doesn't determine everything about a person or their confidence level.

I used to be a perfectionist. I wanted to be the good girl with high grades and had to make sure that everything went perfect. The perfectionism led me to making plans and lists so that I could not forget anything and tick off all the right boxes. I tried to become Miss Perfect, which led to a burnout. After my burnout, I realized that the perfectionism was only a way to control my life and prevent me to fail. But here is the news: there is no ultimate control. Life has unexpected turns, so rather than trying to control all the outcomes, you must learn how to navigate the different outcomes. And life does not need to be perfect, since you do not need to be perfect either.

I've coached many people with low self-esteem who struggle with anxiety. They often try to control their environment to feel comfortable. However, life, especially at work, doesn't always go as planned.

How do you handle situations at work when things get out of hand? Do you panic, or can you step back, assess the situation, and find solutions? As you build confidence and learn to trust yourself in crises, you'll realize you can effectively deal with unexpected challenges. Each time you successfully navigate these situations, your confidence grows, making you better equipped to handle future uncertainties.

If you find yourself often needing everything to be 'just right' to feel at ease, there are several quick and effective strategies you can try:

- Deep breathing exercises: A simple technique like box breathing (inhale for 4 counts, hold for 4, exhale for 4, hold for 4, repeat) can quickly calm your nervous system.

- Mindfulness meditation: Even short daily sessions of 5-10 minutes can help center your thoughts and reduce anxiety. You may notice benefits within a few weeks of regular practice.

- Cognitive-behavioural techniques: Methods like challenging negative thoughts or using positive affirmations can have an impact on your mindset, potentially changing your thought patterns within days or weeks.

These strategies are easily accessible, require no special equipment, and can be practiced almost anywhere. As you use these techniques and build confidence, you may find yourself feeling more at ease even when things don't go exactly as planned.

SOCIAL ENVIRONMENT

Our social environment plays a big role in shaping our confidence. This includes our family and community background, which provide the opportunities and challenges we grow up with. The cultural beliefs around us also matter, as they set certain values and expectations that can affect how confident we feel about different things. Our friends and peers are important too - the people we spend time with can either boost our confidence or make us doubt ourselves.

Another key part of our social environment is our access to resources and support systems. Having opportunities to learn, grow, and succeed can help build confidence. Similarly, having people who believe in us can make a big difference in how we view our own abilities. When our environment doesn't provide enough of these positive elements, it can be harder to develop confidence. However, understanding these influences can help us find ways to build our self-belief, even in challenging circumstances.

For this book, I interviewed Loubna. As a child, she lived in a multicultural environment. When her family moved to a far less diverse area, Loubna, with her Moroccan background, was seen as 'different'. She disliked standing out. In her final year of primary school, after participating in the graduation play, children mocked her for being chubby. This experience led to insecurity, causing Loubna to retreat into books and create her own protective bubble.

However, Loubna's story didn't end there. Through a journey of self-discovery, she learned to love and accept herself fully. She focused on developing her positive qualities and values. Loubna also sought support from mentors and engaged in self-improvement activities. These combined efforts helped her build resilience and overcome past traumas. Today, Loubna is thriving, having transformed her challenges into strengths.

Mental Health Conditions

Conditions such as anxiety, depression, and post-traumatic stress disorder (PTSD) are closely linked to low confidence. They can distort how we see ourselves and the world, causing negative self-talk and reducing our sense of self-worth.

Mental health conditions are complex and usually require an in-depth understanding. For this reason, in this book, specific conditions won't be explored in detail.

Lack of Positive Role Models

Jim Rohn stated: "You are the average of the five people you spend the most time with". Who are your five people? And do they give you energy or deprive you? Do they lift you or push you down? Whom would you most like to be around?

It is important to recognize that we may have developed low self-esteem as a protective mechanism. If you do not display yourself, brag, or stand out you may not be noticed and in some circumstances that may have seemed the best thing to do. Being a confident child may mean going against a dominant parent, so it is safer to keep oneself small.

What is your story? Knowing where your lack of confidence comes from also enables you to identify where your triggers come from. For example, if you feel insecure about your body, looking at perfect bodies on Instagram may trigger your insecurity and, therefore, you might start believing that indeed you should be insecure about your body. In that case, not looking at social media may help because you are avoiding the trigger.

When we are born, we do not have self-awareness yet. That starts to develop when we are between 1,5 to 2 years old. From that age onwards our we become aware, and we develop our 'ego'. The ego refers to the part of the mind responsible for mediating between the conscious and unconscious aspects of personality and is more focused on self-preservation and immediate needs. It controls decision-making and helps us navigate social interactions and maintain self-esteem.

In everyday terms, the ego can be thought of as the "I" or "self" that we present to the world and through which we experience life. While the ego often protects us from dangerous situations, it can sometimes completely take over. We develop our own beliefs and truths, potentially moving away from who we truly are. When we allow our ego to dominate, we might come across as arrogant or cocky. People who are good at reading others can often see past this act and spot the real fears and doubts underneath.

Beneath the ego lies a more authentic version of ourselves, free from societal conditioning and defensive mechanisms: the True Self. This True Self is our essence or core being. To truly embrace self-love, we need to recognize our ego while preventing it from dominating our actions. The ultimate goal is to be and show up as our True Self.

Exercise: Mapping Your Life's Journey

Create a timeline of significant events in your life, both positive and negative. Focus on situations that have had a lasting impact on you. Examine your timeline closely. As you reflect, consider these questions:

- Can you identify any common threads or patterns?

- Is there an overarching theme to your experiences?

- Do you notice any recurring situations or challenges?

- Reflect on how these events have shaped your sense of self:

- How might these experiences have influenced your ego development?

- Can you recognize instances where your ego's protective mechanisms were at play?

- Are there moments where you felt closer to your True Self?

- Consider how this awareness might help you moving forward:

- How can understanding these patterns help you navigate future challenges?

- In what ways can you use this insight to align more closely with your True Self?

When I completed this exercise, I reflected on defining life events: my relationship with my father, my parents' divorce, my burnout, various health issues including surgeries, and other significant experiences. As I examined these events, a common theme emerged: *boundaries*.

I realized I had a pattern of allowing others to cross my personal boundaries. Interesting enough, this pattern manifested physically through endometriosis, a condition where cells from the uterine lining cross boundaries to grow on other organs, in my case, the intestines. This revelation was profound. I understood that a central theme in my life has been learning to establish and maintain healthy boundaries. It became clear that finding the right balance in setting these boundaries is crucial for my personal growth and well-being.

Why some have confidence and others do not?

Given all the above areas that influence self-confidence, it may be clear that this is a difficult question to answer. We are all different and one remark which may influence your life, may not affect someone else's confidence at all.

It is also important to realize that we can have confidence in one area and not in another one. Some people may be insecure about how they look, but very confident in their abilities that they need to do their job. You may recognize some of the aspects that led to you feeling less secure, but rather than remaining stuck in the causes, we want to work on how to move towards high self-esteem and self-love.

CHAPTER 3

How Can You Get More Confidence?

In the previous chapter, we looked at reasons that led to having more or less confidence. Now, we'll examine Maslow's 4-phase model, which I used as a basis for my own model for self-confidence.

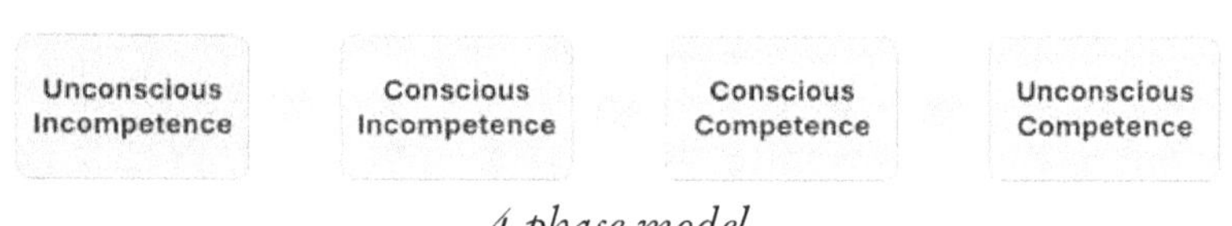

4-phase model

Unconscious Incompetence: In this phase, the individual is not aware of their own deficits; you do not know what you do not know. This is why I explained the many reasons for a lack of self-confidence in Chapter 2, so that you can recognize where it is coming from before you can move to the next stage.

Conscious Incompetence: At this stage, you become aware of areas where your confidence is lacking. You recognize situations or tasks where you feel insecure or inadequate. While you now understand that you need to build your confidence, you're not yet sure how to do it. This awareness is a crucial step in your journey towards self-assurance, as it highlights the specific aspects of confidence you need to work on.

Conscious Competence: In this phase, you attain a level of skill or knowledge through conscious effort and practice. You know how to boost your confidence and feel confident. However, it requires concentration and effort.

Unconscious Competence: In this last stage of the model, competence becomes almost second nature. Individuals can perform the skill effortlessly and without much conscious thought. It becomes ingrained in you, and you can live as the True Self. This is also the stage where you will feel self-love.

If you are anything like I was, you may be looking at others to help you to resolve your issues. If the reason for feeling insecure is due to the lack of love from your parents, then yes, it may be the cause, but the solution is not to think that when they start loving you, the problem will vanish. This way, your own confidence depends on them changing their behaviour. No, the solution must come from inside YOU.

Years ago, I worked at a company where I had to work closely with the legal department. I was used to that aspect from previous jobs, and it had always gone really well. However, this time I encountered serious problems in working with one colleague. She did not appreciate my input and had her own way of working that generated serious delays for the business, which affected our relationship as colleagues. I tried all kinds of ways to improve our relationship, but she questioned my ability to work on legal matters from a commercial side. Eventually, I tried to avoid working with her, but that was not possible given the fact that I needed input from the legal department. After I had exhausted all my other options, I realised that the only way forward was to change myself. I realized that by questioning my abilities this colleague had touched upon a part of me that was not confident enough and self-doubting, and that she was mirroring her own insecurities on me. When I reflected upon that idea further, I realized that although I had no legal background my many years in the field had given me enough knowledge to work on commercial matters. Rather than avoiding her, I explained to my colleague my reasoning behind my input and decided to look at her in a different way. Soon, I noticed she was afraid of failure and was insecure, and that is why she behaved that way. By seeing her in a different light and having compassion for her, slowly our relationship began to improve. We even started to like each other and eventually became a good team.

To assert yourself with confidence, you must recognize and appreciate your own value and contributions. You have unique skills, experiences, and perspectives that can benefit your organization and your clients. Don't let impostor syndrome or self-doubt hold you back from expressing your opinions, sharing your ideas, or taking on new challenges. Remind yourself frequently of your achievements, strengths, and goals, and remember to celebrate your successes.

My friend Johan has been complaining for years about his job and the company he is working for. He often talked about finding another job but was unsure about what he wanted to do. Last year, during another conversation about the same topic, I asked him, "Johann, can you imagine yourself doing this job 5 years from now?" "No!" he said immediately.

Recently I met up with Johan again. He told me that he was still with the same company, but he was much happier now, and described the process of discovering that the answer was inside him. Instead of complaining about the company, he changed his attitude and realized he quite likes his work. By cultivating his confidence, Johan now shows more courage in his work. In contrast to the old him, wondering if he was competent enough, he now knows he's confident and can achieve much better results. By changing his attitude and views, he was able to look at his work and his behaviour in a different way. He stopped the negative self-talk and replaced it with encouraging sentences and positive affirmations.

How can you make a similar change in your own life? I highly recommend two books which will aid with the process of changing your own inner voices: The Choice by Edith Eger and Man's Search For Meaning by Viktor Frankl.

These books have made a big difference in my life, as they show that even under the hardest circumstances (both Edith and Viktor suffered from terrible ordeals during World War 2) we can choose how to act/behave. Instead of feeling a victim, they took control over their thoughts and became creators of their own life. If they can do it under those awful circumstances, then surely, we can manage this in far easier situations.

Dr. Amy Cuddy, a social psychologist and author of Presence: Bringing Your Boldest Self to Your Biggest Challenges, states, "Self-confidence comes from knowing that you have the power to control your own destiny. It's about believing in your ability to shape your future."

Step 1: Mind your Power Word

Exercise: find your power word

Stand up straight, with your legs spread apart about the width of your hips. Focus on the feeling of your feet on the ground, then try to feel each toe on the floor, then your heels. Now breathe in slowly for 4 counts, then breathe out even slower for 6 counts, all the time focusing on the feeling of your feet on the ground. Feel how stable you are, standing with both feet on the ground. Feel your lower legs, feel your upper legs, feel your belly, all while continuing to breathe slowly. Do this for a minute. How did this feel? Do you feel calmer and maybe stronger?

Now take a piece of paper and write down in which areas in your life you feel confident. Be specific! To help you, here are some suggestions:

Social interactions with friends/family/partner

Appearance

Knowledge

Skills in your personal life/work

Languages, etc.

I hope you were able to identify areas where you feel confident. If you're struggling, take a moment to reflect on past achievements and skills you've developed over time. Consider the feedback you've received from others in the past as a guide but focus on recognizing your own strengths from within. Trust in your own judgment to identify what you're good at and where your confidence lies.

Now, close your eyes for a moment and think about the area(s) you feel confident in. Picture specific moments where this confidence was displayed, as if you are replaying a movie in your head. When you see this movie in your mind, notice how it feels. Where do you feel this in your body? Is there a specific area or an overall feeling? Did you feel powerful in that area at that moment? Try to take a mental picture of it, as if you are capturing the moment with a snapshot which includes the bodily feeling too.

If you could describe this moment with one word, what would that word be? Write down that word on a piece of paper and use it as an anchor. Put that piece of paper in a place where you see it several times a day and feel that feeling again, reinforce it. Repeat this as often as possible.

Several years ago, I was with my family in Ölüdeniz, Turkey. The environment there is stunning. The sea is crystal clear, the sand is white, and the mountains surround the beach, creating a breathtaking view. My husband and daughter saw several advertisements for paragliding, and I encouraged them, saying, 'If you ever want to paraglide, do it here, as it is so beautiful.'

As I am afraid of heights, I had no intention of joining them. However, when they signed up, the man behind the reception convinced me that the height would not be scary. Since I knew that one way to increase self-confidence is to expand your comfort zone and overcome fear, I decided to take the leap (literally) and sign up. I was not dressed for the occasion and was wearing flip flops, so one of the instructors lent me his sneakers. They drove us up the hill in a Jeep to get to the starting point, and I began to feel my courage draining away as we ascended. I found a bag of crisps in my purse and frantically ate the whole bag, trying to stave off my nerves.

Before long I was standing at the starting point wearing a full-face helmet with a closed visor, an overall, and borrowed sneakers. Adrenaline spiked through my body. The guy who was doing the jump with me, told me when to run and jump from the hill at the right moment. Instead of falling, we soared into the air with the beach below us. Once in the air, I couldn't help admiring the view—it was so beautiful. The sky was a pure blue without as much as one cloud. The silence and beauty were incredible, and I felt on top of the world.

However, when we started curving to the right, my body swung sideways, and a feeling of nausea appeared. After some gentle rocking, swinging, pitching, and a momentary "free fall" sensation, motion sickness hit me bad. My stomach completely turned upside down. Did I mention the closed visor and the crisps I had eaten? And that below us lay a beautiful beach, covered with sunbathers enjoying their day?

After some time, we landed safely on the ground. I will spare you the details, but I had to hose everything down. I felt embarrassed, but also felt very proud. Looking back, it really was not very scary, and we had a big laugh afterward about this whole situation. To this day, if something very challenging comes my way, I say to myself: PARAGLIDING as a power word, to remind myself that I can do it. A challenge may look daunting, but usually in our minds it is worse than it is in real life.

One of my clients moved to another country to study and did other brave things like changing her field of study and cycling to other countries. When we worked on her power word, she came up with: BADASS.

What is your POWER-WORD?

***

Fear

Do you have dreams, but is fear holding you back from achieving them? Do you believe that once you are confident that you will not be fearful again?

Unfortunately, that is not true. Being confident does not mean there is no fear. Even very successful people feel fear regularly! However, one of the most powerful traits that successful people have, is the ability to respond confidently despite the presence of fear. Their desire to achieve their dream becomes greater than the fear that comes with the challenges of achieving it.

Fear is there to protect you and in many cases this emotion is very helpful. If you touch the hot stove and burn your hand, the next time fear will warn you not to touch it, protecting you from another injury. But we also carry a lot of fear that is unnecessary and is actually holding us back.

Let us have a look at FOMO—the so-called fear of missing out—which is something that a lot of people feel. They need to check social media very often to prevent them from missing out on something. But ask yourself: what would you be missing out on? And would that be something important? I coach several young women who suffer from this a lot. However, when they do not look at social media for a few days, they notice that nothing happened, and they did not miss anything important.

Fear is quite often related to a limited belief. For example:" I am afraid to ask for that promotion because I do not have experience enough for that job. I am afraid to speak up to the manager as he has a much higher rank than I have. I am not taking a risk by making a deal for this very innovative product because it may fail."

Self-confidence and fear are closely linked to each other. When you do not feel confident, a lot of situations seem fearful, and we tend to make up the worst scenarios in our minds. Often, we are better at doing this than the best screenplay writer, and we begin to believe the fear is real.

Sometimes fear is functional, e.g. when you must pitch for a huge client or do an important purchase or an exam, you may feel nervousness and fear. In these scenarios, fear helps you to function even better due to the adrenaline it is producing.

Is fear the best advisor? Well in some cases it is but, in many cases, not so much. Fear often falls into the perceived 'psychological threat' camp—usually a result of culture, uncertainty, feelings of isolation or difficult relationships.

Years ago, I worked for a consulting company and the female founder was not an easy one to work with. One of the colleagues had made a mistake and she wanted me to address this to the client in a very unpleasant way. I did not feel comfortable doing it and it was against my own values, but she was the founder and could make or break my career. I did as she asked me to do, as I feared the consequences. But afterwards I felt awful, and I made myself a promise: I will not do anything anymore that goes against my own values and beliefs for an employer. Looking back: what was I afraid for? That she would fire me? And if so, what would be the worst thing that could happen? That I had to look for another job? Even in that worst case scenario, I would have felt better as I would have been true to myself. Although I had many cases at work where I was put in a similar position, I was never disloyal to myself again (and by the way, I was never fired for pushing back. In fact, when I explained my reasoning, they usually understood and even respected me for it).

What would your dream business, job or life look like if fear was out of the way? Ask yourself truthfully, is that fear realistic, or is it overprotective and holding you back?

How can you overcome some of that fear? You could try to EXPAND your comfort zone. Step by step, move towards that fear that is holding you back. If you want to be a performer but are afraid of being on stage, you might start by telling a story to a group of friends, then stand up at a network event and give a presentation for a small group. If needed, you can educate yourself to become better and learn the tools that will help you gain more confidence. In time the fear will soften its voice, until it only whispers in your ear. Then you may say, 'Thanks, I know you are protecting me but, in this case, you do not need to. I've got this.'

You, as a complete human being, are much more powerful than your fear alone. Often, we let fear run the complete show, including the lights and the stage. So rather than saying: 'I am afraid', you can say: 'PART of me is afraid.' When we realize that fear is only part of who we are, it is easier to see that we have so many more parts. We need to shift our relationship with fear. We grow our confidence when we choose faith over fear and take action.

Over time, we become less and less prone to fear and more able to have confidence.

How many decisions are not taken at work, how many faults not reported, how many issues not mentioned because of fear? How many burnouts are caused by fear?

Fear of Failure

Fear of failure is an important source of anxiety, particularly in the workplace. And failure is inevitable, since we are human and sometimes, we make mistakes. Employees may worry about making mistakes or not meeting their targets, which can paralyze them, hinder their professional growth, and prevent them and the company from taking necessary risks to innovate and grow.

Back in the days at the office when I made a mistake, I would tell myself over and over again that I was stupid, and I would be really harsh on myself. But I also realized over time that failure is almost never fatal. And guess what? After a while, you forget you made a mistake. This might be because the mistake was an opportunity to grow, and it might help to implement something that helps you not to repeat that same mistake again.

Making mistakes is inevitable. When we look at history, we see that often the best innovations come from previous failures (e.g., penicillin, post-it Notes, and pacemakers). The more interesting question is: why are we afraid to fail? I believe this has to do with the possible consequences that failure has and the feelings we link to those potential consequences.

In companies, many employees fear retaliation. A mistake can lead to a bad appraisal or, even worse, to being fired. However, this fear might actually cause more mistakes as we try so hard not to make any mistakes and try to fit in so hard. As an entrepreneur, failures can lead to losing money or even to losing the business. But fear feeds self-doubt. We need to overcome fear in order to be brave and become successful. Accept that you will make mistakes and that you cannot be good at everything (nor all the time). If you are willing to learn from them, even better.

Dr. Carol Dweck, writer of Mindset: The New Psychology of Success states, "The view you adopt for yourself profoundly affects the way you lead your life. Believing that your qualities are carved in stone—the fixed mindset—creates an urgency to prove yourself over and over."

Job insecurity is a concern for many employees. They may worry about layoffs, downsizing, or their positions becoming obsolete. This fear can lead to chronic stress and decreased job satisfaction. My husband has been working for a huge multinational company, and he has already 'survived' 15 restructurings of the company. This stress has definitely had its impact on him over the years, but at the same time, it has helped him to become resilient.

When you are an entrepreneur, you may be afraid to lose your company. I have been there, too, since my first company was not successful. Does that make me a failure? No, it gave me the opportunity to do it better the next time.

*"Change the way you look at things, and things
will look differently".*

Because of the situation at home and the fact that there were always discussions about money, I did not go to college straight after high school and instead started a job as a secretary. That way I could earn money and do various studies in the evening. While working as an executive secretary for a multinational company, I noticed that in comparison to the employees that had a university degree, I was treated differently. This made me feel insecure, as if I was not smart enough or did not belong due to the absence of a degree. And at the same time, I felt an internal resistance to that idea, telling me that I was just as worthy as the ones with a degree. That motivated me to study for degrees in the evenings, and at a certain point, I bid farewell to my job as a secretary and started another job. What I did not know at the new job, I would learn by working hard and by learning from others. I had already adapted a growth-mindset.

It felt powerful to work on other projects and be assigned responsibility. Had I changed? No. It was the perception of me—and the one that I believed others had of me—that had changed and helped me to gain more confidence. And though currently I hold two degrees, I realize now that it is not the diplomas that give confidence. It is the change within me.

We often give our power away to others, especially when we believe that we know how they feel about us and relate our own confidence to that. But are other people really thinking that way about you? How can you possibly know this for sure?

It is also a way to move responsibility away from us. So that we can say: it is the other's fault, and they should change or do this or do that so that we can feel better. If you do not get along with a co-worker, you may think that the solution is to avoid that colleague or start working somewhere else. However, the problem is that when we do not resolve our issues, they will come back to us, maybe in the form of another co-worker at another company. The solution is inside us.

Step 2: Mind Yourself

Our identities are formed by many factors, such as where we are born, how we are raised, our social class, and our physical appearance. They are even more impacted by our limiting beliefs. What have we been told, and do we truly believe these things? Beliefs can restrain us and keep us smaller than we really are, and when we believe they are true, they become self-fulfilling prophecies. The universe works in such a way that if you truly believe something, you will encounter situations that seem to confirm it. It's as if the universe is responding to your beliefs with, "Your wish is my command."

Exercise: Identify Your Identity

What is your identity? Please write down on a piece of paper who and/or what you think you are.

The thing is that if we say, for example, 'I am a businesswoman', then you identify yourself as one. This applies for everything where we say: I am this, I am that, I am...

One of my clients told me she felt 'invisible at work'. I asked her if she actually saw and recognized herself, and she had to admit that no, she didn't. I wondered how she can expect anyone to see and recognize her when she did not even see herself. This client put on one of the designer dresses from my former business and started crying, because she felt strong for the first time and truly saw herself. A few months later she sent me an email and told me she had been promoted.

When you are not feeling worthy at work and you do not speak up during meetings, most people do not see you and that by itself seems to confirm to you are not worthy. But as the example above shows, it works the other way around, too.

Now, what if the situations we encounter are not there to confirm our beliefs but invite us to have a closer look at them?

To face our challenges, we need to step out of our comfort zone, which I like to call a 'jump'. Many people only jump once there is a very bad situation that forces them to respond. How would it be if we can avoid those situations by jumping beforehand? And having the courage to expand our comfort zones already when we do not need to but want to?

There are moments in life when you feel you just have to jump.

When I look back at my youth, I see my urge to get out of my parents' house. At the age of 20, I married a guy I had been seeing at school for several years. Looking back, I do not even know if I was in love with him, but I was so insecure that having attention from someone felt lovely. Before the wedding, I knew it was a mistake, but I did not have the confidence to break up and I was preoccupied with what others would say and think and the embarrassment this would bring to us both. I bit my tongue, and the wedding went ahead. After a year, I clearly felt that we did not have a good marriage and I felt very unhappy. Soon after our wedding, I became ill and had to have bowel surgery (life was telling me something...) and the recovery was tough. We divorced after one year of marriage. My ex-husband was not a bad guy, but we were young and did not bring out the best in each other, and we were still figuring out our own identities. Also, due to his own uncertainty, there was focus on my shortcomings, which made my self-confidence diminish even further. Leaving him was one of the best decisions I ever made. It made me realize that I could build on my own happiness and that helped me to grow my confidence. Shortly after the divorce, I met my current husband, Frans.

It's important to look at situations we come across as opportunities to become more aware of ourselves and our beliefs, as well as examining how these beliefs might hold us back. Some of the beliefs may have served and protected us in the past, but do they still serve us today?

When caught up in your identity, it feels like it defines you completely. You may think you ARE your identity, but it's only a part of you. Who are you without it? You are still you. In reality, you have an identity; it doesn't have you. Your identity is just one part of your larger self. While identity refers to how we define and perceive ourselves, often shaped by our roles and experiences, ego is the part of our psyche that creates a sense of self-importance and can lead to attachment to these identities, potentially limiting our growth and self-awareness. In this context, identity can be seen as broader than ego, as it encompasses all aspects of how we define ourselves, while ego is a specific psychological construct that interacts with and sometimes clings to these identities. Understanding this distinction can help us recognize when we're overly attached to certain aspects of our identity and open the door to personal growth.

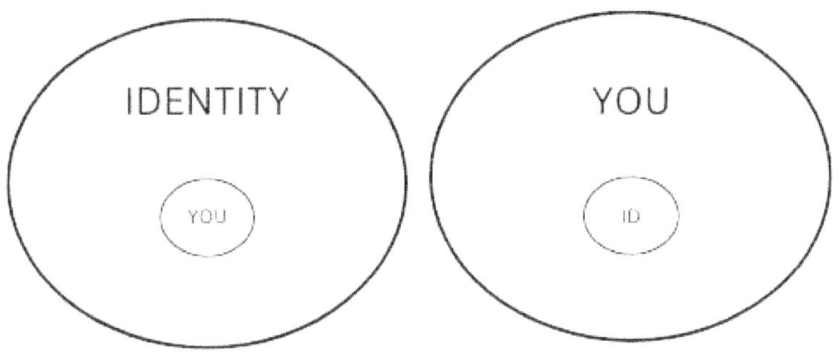

In 2003, my husband was offered a job in London. Our daughter was only 8 years old then, and although I had a great job, we decided to move abroad. We sold our house and moved to the UK. My husband went to work, and my daughter went to school, and there I was, alone. One of the first things I noticed was that a huge part of my identity came from my job at Unilever and the things I did there. This was an invite to look deeper inside as to what this veil of identity actually was. It was indeed a veil and nothing more, and its absence did not change who I was or what I was worth. I did learn, though, that because I was good at my work, there was now less appreciation. Did that make me suddenly worthless? No, it did not. But, in all honesty, I had to go through that first. I literally felt as if all my clothes had been taken off me, and I was standing there naked and unshielded.

I always had wanted to study fashion design, so I decided to study in the UK. At first, I was not admitted as the university year had already started, but after a lot of calls and persuasion from my side, I was asked to come and show my portfolio. I had no such thing but compiled a few things together, and I was admitted. In class, I was one of the oldest students. In hindsight I am so glad I did not study there in my early twenties, as I do not think I would have had enough resilience to cope with the way some of the teachers taught us to compete and to keep up with the rest of the students. But I worked very hard and got to know a very nice fellow student, and together we eventually graduated with first-class honours. The work I did during my degree increased my resilience, which in turn boosted my confidence.

One of my friends used to be a famous weightlifter and was even called 'the strongest woman' of her country. She trained very hard and was nominated for the Olympic games. Unfortunately, she suffered a severe sports injury and could not be a top athlete anymore. Because of this, she went through an identity crisis: who was she without the training, without the events, without the praise from the public, without the achievements in her sport? At first, she felt like a failure. But after a while, she was able to overcome this. Currently she is a very successful leadership trainer and helps to empower others. What helped her? Having a mentor and people around her who believed in her and knew she was much more than just an athlete.

CHAPTER 4

Unconscious Incompetence

The first phase of the model of 4 stages of competence is *Unconscious Incompetence*. This is the step where you are not aware of your lack of skill and lack of proficiency; you do not know what you do not know.

Based on examples and explanations of the previous chapters, we may have concluded that what we are experiencing is caused by a lack of self-esteem and self-love. In this stage, we are still ignorant. This is the phase where we have low self-confidence and do not love ourselves enough.

Now before we dig into that, let us make a distinction between confidence, self-worth, and love. As you may think that it is all the same and it is not.

SELF CONFIDENCE

Self-confidence is the belief in one's abilities to accomplish tasks and overcome challenges. Depending on the situation and external feedback, it can fluctuate. Self-confidence:

- Is focused on specific skills or competencies.

- Can be developed through practice, experience, and positive reinforcement.

- Is often influenced by external validation and comparison with others.

- May lead to success in certain areas but not necessarily fulfilment or happiness.

- Can be built through setting and achieving goals, facing fears, and taking risks.

- May lead to feelings of inadequacy or impostor syndrome in the absence of external validation.

- Is often associated with assertiveness and taking initiative.

- Can coexist with low self-worth or self-love if based solely on external achievements.

From this, we can clearly see and conclude that there is a dependency between something or someone outside of us and self-confidence. The fact is, however, that no matter how often someone tells you that you are worthy or okay, if you do not believe it yourself, it will not stick.

SELF-WORTH

Self-Worth:

- Is the intrinsic value and belief in oneself regardless of external achievements or validation.

- Remains relatively stable and consistent, not easily swayed by external factors.

- Is not necessarily tied to accomplishments or skills but rather to inherent value as a person.

- Is developed through recognizing and honouring one's own worthiness.

- Is less affected by external opinions or comparisons with others.

- Provides a foundation for healthy relationships and boundaries.

- May require inner work and healing from past experiences that have affected self-worth.

- Is less likely to be affected by failure or criticism, because sense of worth isn't based on outside factors.

- Provides a sense of inner security and stability, even in the face of uncertainty.

- Can be cultivated through practices such as self-compassion, gratitude, and mindfulness.

Self-worth is much more inward and not dependent on factors outside us.

SELF-LOVE

Self-love:

- Is a deep appreciation and acceptance of oneself, including flaws and imperfections.

- Often grows stronger with self-awareness and self-compassion practices.

- Extends beyond individual traits or achievements to encompass the whole self.

- Is nurtured through acts of self-care, compassion, and forgiveness.

- Is rooted in an internal sense of fulfilment and contentment.

- Forms the basis for healthy self-esteem and resilience in the face of challenges.

- Flourishes in environments that prioritize authenticity and self-expression, allowing for vulnerability and openness without fear of rejection or judgment, and supporting healthy boundaries and self-respect in relationships.

- Is essential for overall well-being and fulfilment, influencing all aspects of life.

Self-love goes even deeper than self-worth and is much more stable than confidence. It is what we strive for, and the funny thing is, is that we already have it, but our beliefs are or have been in the way.

For now, we will focus on increasing self-confidence and being aware of what happens, what our triggers are, and how we can work on this.

A study by the Harvard Business Review found that employees with high self-confidence are more likely to be promoted and take on leadership roles. Confidence is linked to better job performance, higher job satisfaction, and improved interpersonal relationships at work.

Years ago, there was an TV commercial with a funny man that had a mini person on each of his shoulders. One was a naughty, daring one and the other one was an angel. They were talking to him and depending on which voice spoke the loudest, he either behaved very bravely or very naughty. According to Positive Intelligence, we all have saboteurs and sages talking to us. What kind of voices are talking to you? We have several, and some talk louder than others. They may be there to protect us and help us to overcome challenges by encouraging us.

While writing this book, I asked several people how confidence evolved and what it was that helped them. One story came from one of my best friends. She was raised in a family where she was never praised or told that what she did was good. Her mother was insecure too. All this resulted in her feeling (and telling herself) she was not good enough. She believed that no matter what she did or would do, she would never ever be good enough. At school, they told her, "Please be vocal because we also want to hear your voice", which increased her low esteem because it seemed like a confirmation that she was indeed different (not good enough). She had a university degree but did not feel that the subject she had studied was something that would be taken seriously or esteemed as a good degree, therefore she hardly mentioned it. She was insecure about how she looked, who she was, about her life, and so on. Because of her deep questions about life, her father often told her not to be so "difficult". At work, she got praised for what she did but did not really believe it. She would not allow the compliments to sink in as she was so convinced that she was not enough.

One day she had to give a keynote speech to a group of highly educated people, and it was so good that she got a standing ovation. When she told her mum about it, her mother told her not to speak about this as it would make her sound arrogant. My friend even took a job for which she was overqualified as she believed that it was the only job she was able to get. To cover her insecurity, she became a perfectionist and tried to control her work. After a burnout, she got to know the work of Dr. Joe Dispenza and through these teachings she realized that she was so much more than just the mind and her limited beliefs. In combination with embodiment, this led her to gain confidence. Of course, it did not happen overnight, but nowadays she truly loves herself and accepts what and who she is. The one thing she said was, "if only I had known before, I would not have wasted so much energy on feeling insecure."

Step 3: Mind your Inner Voices

Exercise: Identify Your Voices

Let's have some fun. Observe how you are talking to yourself and to others about yourself. For example, imagine there is a new project at work that requires you to organize a big event. You have never done that before, so do you believe that you can do it, or do you tell yourself and others that you are not the right person, because you are not creative or good enough to do this?

For the coming period, observe the voices within you. Listen to what they say and write down their messages on post-it notes, using a new note for each sentence. For example: "I can never do this," "I am not slim enough," "They will find out I'm not capable of this job," etc. Make sure you also write the positive voices on post-it notes too.

Pretend you are in a movie and are observing what these voices tell you. At first, you may not notice them, but bit by bit, you will become more aware of these characters.

Once you have accumulated these post-it notes, try to group and name them. For example, there might be one voice that constantly exaggerates, which you might call the 'drama queen.' There might also be an 'empowering' voice that helps you overcome challenges. Write the name of each voice on a separate post-it note. Take a large piece of paper and turn it landscape. At the top of the page, list the names of the voices horizontally, and below each name, add the corresponding post-it notes with the things they are telling you.

Name of voice (e.g. dramaqueen)	Name of voice (e.g. Empowervoice)	Name of voice (e.g. the Pleaser)	Name of voice (e.g. the Perfectionist)	Name of voice (e.g. the Lazy one)	Name of voice (e.g. the Rookie)	Name of voice	Name of voice
Eg. you will never ever be able to get a promotion	Eg: you can do anything you want	...	....	...	...	...	...
...	....	...	...	...	...		
...	....	...	...	...	...		
...	....	...	...	...	...		

Give as many examples or names as come up. There is no right or wrong, and please do not *judge*. Just *observe* what these voices are telling you. Make it fun, as if you are looking at your favourite movie. Observe the characters and what they are saying, how they speak. Are they loud or silent, do they speak fast or slow? But even more importantly: how do those characters make you **feel**?

Once you are done (and this is a work in progress and not ready instantly), have a look at what you are telling yourself. Is it reinforcing? Are you talking in a negative way to yourself and are there more negative sentences than positive? Have compassion, do not beat yourself up over the things you are thinking. Do not be judgmental about it, since this is the first time you are aware of the things you are believing. We will continue working on this, so please save your paper with the post-it notes.

Please go to https://www.confidenceatwork.nl/resources/and download the worksheet.

If the "judge" in you looks at the paper and tells you that you are crazy with all those voices, just let it go. Everybody has those voices. The thing is, however, that we are not always aware of them. And because some voices are so loud, we cannot hear the ones that whisper. So, usually, the ones that heard more often are the ones we act upon. This is exactly why we can feel as if we are not happy or satisfied, because we do not acknowledge all voices and tend to give our power to the ones that shout loudest.

When Peter was taking a sabbatical from work, he noticed that his line manager was talking about this to others a lot and he did not like this. However, one of his voices told him not to pay attention to this feeling. One day a colleague came to him and started mentioning that he had heard about Peter's upcoming sabbatical. Peter was so irritated, and the voice he tried to silence became louder and louder. When we sat down together, I asked him how it would be if he would listen to that voice rather than repressing it and talk to this line manager to express his feelings. Peter took my advice and discovered that the line manager did not mean anything by mentioning it (except that he aspired to take a sabbatical too) and the air was cleared.

Do you have examples where a voice that is not heard or seen, starts talking louder and louder to you till you break down over something that may not be very important? Congratulations: we all have! You are completely normal and human. The things that those voices say to us are actually limited beliefs. And we are full of them. In fact, quite often they run the movie of our life.

Now have a look at your sheet again: which voices are helping you and which ones are limiting you?

On my path to personal development, I joined a course on personal effectiveness. One of the exercises was to envision a dream of what you want to be and how you want your career to look. For years, I dreamed of becoming an entrepreneur and starting my own business, but I had not achieved it yet. For this exercise, we had to sit on the floor with one person standing in front of us, representing our dream, and another behind us, representing the obstacles holding us back. We had to move towards the person in front of us, whilst the person behind us would literally try to prevent us from moving forward.

There I was, sitting on the floor. I looked at my dream in front of me and knew I had to move towards it. But I did NOTHING. I didn't even attempt to move. I had given up on my dream and did not know how to move forward. Why? Because so many voices were holding me back, talking about the risks of being self-employed, the financial insecurity, and other limiting beliefs. It was a shock to realize that I didn't even want to pursue my dream anymore. Strangely enough, this revelation empowered me. Recognizing how my beliefs were holding me back made me determined to overcome them. A few months later, I did start my own business. Today, I still run that business, helping other companies and employees achieve greater happiness and better results.

How often in our careers have we given up already because we listened and gave all power to those voices that are limiting beliefs?

Anna was one of the first very successful women in trading. She was working for a small company and earned a lot of money for the company and her clients. Anna created a plan on how to help the company earn even more money, but in return she wanted to become a partner in the company. When she proposed the plan, she was laughed at, and the male bosses told her she could never become a partner. One week later, her male colleague—whose plan was nowhere near as good as hers—was promoted to partner. Can you imagine what went on in Anna's head afterwards? The voice in her head told her things like, 'see you are not good enough' and 'you will never make it in this world'. However, one of her voices told her, 'Enough, they do not deserve me' and after listening to that voice, Anna left the company. Nowadays she is on the board of an international bank and has enjoyed a very successful career.

This example shows how limited beliefs can be planted in our minds and how—if we do not listen to them—they stop limiting us. In the next chapter, we will go deeper into those limited beliefs and what you can do to overcome them.

Limited beliefs and boundaries are connected and impact each other. Our beliefs can limit what we think is possible, and without confidence, it's hard to push past those limits or set good boundaries.

For example, if we don't think we deserve love, we might let people treat us badly in relationships. At work, it's important to set limits on things like answering emails after hours or working weekends.

By challenging our limiting beliefs and setting clear boundaries, we can be more authentic and empower ourselves. This helps us value ourselves and grow. My dear friend Hannie Wiering shows this so clearly in her 'GENIUS MODEL ©'.

The Geniusmodel

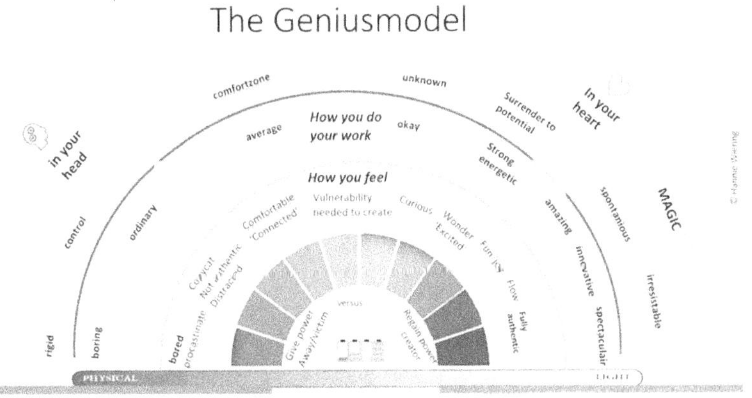

This model is called 'The Genius', to emphasize that we are capable of much more than we think. That we are self-regulating and can bring ourselves into any state we desire. That we ourselves have this power, regardless of external circumstances. When we give our power away (see left side) and function mainly from the head our performance will be average at best (and as the model shows, our energy is depicted as well). We may feel bored, may act rigidly, desire control and are mainly operating from our head. On the other hand, once we function from the heart and connect the heart and mind together, we can regain our power. We can charge our battery, become curious, have fun and create flow and eventually, produce magic. We surrender to our potential (and do not let the limited beliefs hold us back). But first we need confidence to step into our magnificence.

Let us now go deeper into boundary-setting. Boundaries are like personal guidelines or limits that we establish to protect our well-being, time, and resources. They help define what is acceptable and what is not in our interactions with others and in our own behaviours. Setting boundaries involves recognizing and respecting your own needs, values, and limitations, as well as communicating them clearly to others. In that respect, we can distinguish overperformers and underperformers.

OVERPERFORMERS

When we don't have clear boundaries, we often push ourselves too hard, trying to please everyone. We might think this will make us feel better about ourselves, but it's a trap. Sure, getting praise feels good at first, but if we depend on others to make us feel worthy, we're never really satisfied. It's like there's a void inside us that we're trying to fill with other people's approval. But no matter how much praise we get, that void stays empty. We keep chasing more and more validation, setting impossible standards for ourselves.

This cycle is exhausting. We might start feeling insecure, doubting ourselves, or thinking we're not good enough when we can't meet these crazy expectations. Eventually, we burn out. And then we feel guilty for burning out, which makes us feel even worse about ourselves. It's a vicious circle, and it all starts with not having strong boundaries and not believing in our own worth.

In the weeks before being diagnosed with burnout, I was sitting on the floor and playing with my daughter when I heard my daughter say, "Mummy, please wake up." I was so tired that I had fallen asleep whilst playing with her. That was the moment I realized that something was very wrong, and I had to see a doctor. I also felt a total failure for not even being able to play with my daughter.

In therapy, one of the first questions I was asked was, 'where are your limits?' I really could not answer that question, simply because I never thought about this. I always felt I should stretch and stretch, constantly striving for more. In doing so, I put my mind over my body. Do you recognize this feeling in yourself?

After 4 months of intensive therapy, I could move properly again and felt so different. They taught me to recognize the language of my body and to listen to it closely. The greatest lesson was that I had to speak up and set boundaries and realize that by doing so, people would not suddenly stop loving or liking me. In fact, soon I realized that relationships became easier because I was upfront about how I felt and what I needed to be okay.

While overperformers push themselves beyond healthy limits, there's another group that struggles with boundaries in a different way: underperformers. Both groups have difficulty with boundary-setting, but the manifestation is quite different.

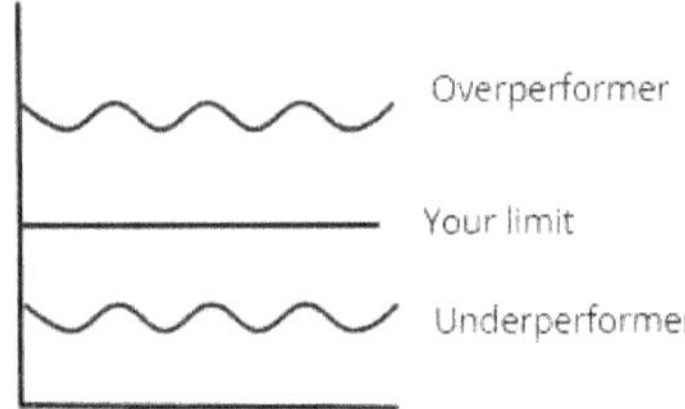

UNDERPERFORMERS

Unlike overperformers who constantly work above the baseline, underperformers can always see the limit or boundary (as shown in the picture above) but struggle to reach it. If we have trouble setting boundaries or asserting ourselves, we may find ourselves consistently underperforming. This could be due to a fear of failure, a lack of self-belief, or difficulty prioritizing our own needs amidst external demands.

Just as with overperformers, this pattern can erode self-confidence. When we repeatedly neglect our own needs or fail to assert ourselves, it reinforces a belief that we are not capable or worthy of success. The key difference is that while overperformers burn out from doing too much, underperformers may feel stuck and unfulfilled from not reaching their potential.

Transgressive behaviour

Confidence and setting boundaries become even more important in cases of transgressive behaviour, where socially accepted standards of behaviour, belief, morality, or taste are violated or challenged. When people feel secure in themselves and their abilities, they are more likely to set healthy boundaries, assert themselves, and maintain a sense of self-respect. Conversely, a lack of confidence can lead to boundary issues, as individuals may struggle to advocate for their needs and desires.

Transgressive behaviour often arises because of boundary violations, either by oneself or others. This can manifest in various forms, from people-pleasing and overcommitting to outright rebellion against societal norms. Interestingly, confidence plays a crucial role in how individuals respond to transgressions. Those with a strong sense of self are more likely to assert their boundaries firmly and resist engaging in behaviours that compromise their values. I am not saying that we should accept or can prevent transgressive behaviour, nor that it will never happen again, but with increased self-esteem you will be more likely to respond in a way that reduces the chances of it going on, as you have the courage and assertiveness to speak up and the self-worth to realize you are not causing this.

Boundary setting

Setting boundaries is a fundamental aspect of self-care and personal development. It involves defining what is acceptable and unacceptable in one's interactions and relationships. Confidence empowers you to establish and maintain these boundaries effectively, fostering healthier connections with others and promoting emotional well-being.

When I look back at events that happened in my life, I realized that every single one of them had to do with learning to set healthy boundaries. When I worked at a big international firm as a secretary for the board, I loved to design my own clothes and had made a beautiful skirt (not too short and not too long). One day I entered the boardroom and the CEO said in front of everyone, 'what a horny skirt you are wearing.' I felt awful but went out of the door without saying anything. I cannot believe now that I did not respond to his vile words. I think that if I had been more confident, my energy would have been different and I like to hope that he would not have dared to say it, and if he had, I immediately would have responded in a way that made him realize the inappropriateness of this comment.

During my time at another company, I entered a room to deliver some papers and the head of sales grabbed both of my breasts. I was so overwhelmed and stunned that I froze and eventually walked out of the room without saying anything. I did, however, go to the CEO a few days later and told him about the situation. 'Well, Karina,' the CEO said, 'this man brings in so much money for the company that we will leave this for what it is and there will be no action from us towards him.'

I left the company shortly after that event. Times are fortunately different now (or at least I hope so). In many companies, there are now confidants to go to in these situations, and such terrible behaviour will not go unpunished. But still, we need to set boundaries and have the confidence to speak up to deal with these kinds of situations.

Once I realized that setting healthy boundaries was clearly a theme in my life, I decided to work on my confidence around them. Recurring events that tested my boundaries—as well as transgressive behaviour from others—did not return, or at least not as clearly. Apparently, that was a lesson I had to learn the hard way.

What are you willing to put up with and what not? What *feels* okay and what does not? You know deep within you what you want and what you don't want; it is about getting in touch with that inner feeling again, which we can achieve through embodiment. Bringing our body, mind, and soul in connection with each other again helps us create a sense of fuller embodiment. I like to achieve this state by practising yoga, walking in nature, and meditation, but for you, that might be something else, like listening to music, doing sports, etc.

*'We cannot always change what happens, but
we can change how we respond to it'.*

Chapter 5

Conscious Incompetence

In this chapter, you will gain awareness of your triggers and work on transforming limiting beliefs into empowering ones. The chapter also introduces practices for increasing mindfulness and achieving heart coherence to bridge the gap between mind and heart intelligence.

Step 4: Mind your Beliefs and Believers

In Chapter 4, you created an overview of the voices that are talking to you and divided them into empowering and disempowering categories. Have a look at the different sentences you wrote down.

How do they make you feel? Look at the empowering ones and be grateful for what these voices say to you.

Exercise: 4 Questions

Now, have a close look at one of the disempowering sentences that stand out for you. Let us assume that this voice told you, 'you are stupid.' Then let us use the work of the incredible Byron Katie and apply her 4 questions to this sentence:

1. Is it true? Only reply with a yes or no answer.

2. Can you absolutely know that it's true? Answer this question only if you said yes to question 1.

3. How do you react, what happens, when you believe that thought?

4. Who would you be without the thought?

Then, let us apply the following analysis to the same statement, 'you are stupid':

Is it true? This question invites you to examine the validity of the statement. Upon reflection, you may realize that labelling someone as "stupid" is subjective and based on personal opinions rather than objective truth. Therefore, it's challenging to definitively say that the statement is true for everyone in all circumstances. And if you answered this with a yes: you are believing lies.

Can you absolutely know that it's true? If you answered question 1 with NO, you can skip this question. Here, you're encouraged to consider whether there's any absolute certainty in the statement. Reflecting on the diverse range of abilities, experiences, and perspectives, it becomes evident that the label "stupid" lacks the universality and certainty required for absolute truth.

How do you react, what happens, when you believe that thought? This question invites you to explore the emotional and behavioural consequences of believing the statement. Believing that you are "stupid" may lead to feelings of stress, inadequacy, sadness. It might even lead to situations where you are not even trying anymore because you believe people find you stupid anyway.

Who would you be without the thought? This question encourages you to envision how you would perceive yourself without the judgmental label of "stupid." How would you live? What would you do other than what you currently do?

By applying these four questions, you can gain insights into the nature of your thoughts and beliefs, ultimately leading to greater understanding, empathy, and personal growth.

In addition, think about what this belief has already cost you and how it makes you feel. Think about all the missed opportunities in work and in relationships because you believed you were stupid. I invite you not to skip this part, no matter how uncomfortable, and keep on reading. Please pause and consider if there were situations where you were afraid to speak up because you thought you were not smart enough, or maybe not even worthy. Go back in time, think about it, and write it down.

One of my clients always got nervous when he had to present his reports to people, and even more so to people he did not know.

When I asked him why, he told me that it was because he was afraid that they would start shouting at him. This pathway had already been ingrained in his brain, because in his youth, his father would shout at him after he had spoken up and shared his opinion.

Every time a new report needed to be presented, his old 'voice' told him that people would start shouting at him. Can you imagine how he must have felt every time he had to do this? So, I asked him, 'Did it ever happen that someone shouted at you when presenting the report?" The answer, of course, was no. For years, he suffered from this fear and lack of confidence, but by using the steps from this book, he was finally able to let go of this belief.

Using above 4 questions and looking at the page with the post-it notes (voices), we can see clearly that these voices often tell you things that are not true. And you heard that so often, that you have been believing what these voices say, whereas above by answering the questions it is clear you were believing lies.

Our old, limiting beliefs are often based on misconceptions or negative experiences that we've internalized as truths. If we can accept these false beliefs, we can also choose to adopt new, more positive beliefs that serve us better.

Exercise: Replace Disempowering Beliefs

Let's try an exercise: Take that mental post-it note that says "I am stupid" and replace it with one that says, "I am capable of learning and growth". This isn't about lying to yourself, but about challenging your old assumptions and opening yourself up to new possibilities.

When you start believing in your capacity for growth and intelligence, you'll likely act and behave differently. This new belief becomes a self-fulfilling prophecy, encouraging you to take on challenges and learn from your experiences.

Remember, this new belief isn't a lie - it's an acknowledgment of your potential and an invitation to grow. Everyone has the capacity to learn and improve, and recognizing this in yourself is the first step towards realizing your full potential.

There is a beautiful story that shows the power of belief. An 11-year-old boy was sent home from school because his teachers said he was difficult and stupid. In addition, he was also ill quite often, so his mother decided to homeschool the boy. She never told him that others found him stupid; instead, she told him he was intelligent. The mother did not only teach him subjects like mathematics and history. No, she taught him how to think for himself and not to be afraid of failing. The boy did not think there was such a thing as failure, since he saw everything as a chance to learn.

One day, when he was 16 and working at a railroad station selling newspapers, he rescued a girl. She had fallen on the train tracks and a train was coming. The boy jumped on the tracks and saved the child. The father of the girl was so grateful that he offered the boy a job. Soon he noticed that the boy learned very quickly. By the time this boy was 25, he had already invented more than 400 things. His name was Thomas Edison, and he became one of the most famous inventors ever known.

How different his life would have been if his mother had told him he was stupid. Would he have had the courage to 'think' and see everything as a chance to learn?

Please look at your post-it notes again. How do you feel when you believe all the disempowering voices? Thank them for protecting you during a time in your life when they served a purpose but understand that they now hinder your ability to achieve your goals. If you want to gain confidence and not be held back in your career and life by those voices, please do the above analysis exercise with each one of these voices. Ask yourself the four questions for each of the post-it notes, then rewrite them in a positive and empowered way and in the present tense (I am this/that, etc.).

Although I am all for positivity, be realistic. If one of the sentences says you are a lousy football player, please do not replace it with 'you are the best football player in the world'. However, you can replace it with 'I enjoy playing football and have fun while doing so'. It's important that you keep rephrasing the sentences until they feel empowering and positive.

Which one of the sentences was the hardest to change? And have you been able to change it? If so, please have a look at what you have written.

For this purpose, we take the example of the sentence: where we changed the wording of 'I am stupid' into 'I am smart'. Now let us use this as your affirmation. How does it feel when you say that out loud? Check in with your body and sense if you feel it in a specific place, or if you experience some sensations. Make a note of those.

Place several post-it notes with this sentence at places where you often go, e.g. on the mirror in your bathroom. Or maybe you want to take a picture of it and assign it as your phone's wallpaper or home screen so that every time you see it, you are reminded that you are smart. Use this as your affirmation (as often as possible) and make sure you are naming it in present time and say it out loud. Practice that for at least 21 days every day (it takes a minimum of three weeks to create a new habit and, in this case, a belief). As we have heard the voices say 'you are stupid' so often it may even take longer. Believe you are smart and whenever something happens that may cause you to believe that you are indeed stupid, observe the things you are saying and remind yourself of things that you did well and were actually smart and not stupid.

Please go to https://www.confidenceatwork.nl/resources/ and download the worksheet.

GRATITUDE

By the time you have reached this part of the book, I am convinced that you are making progress and believe in your progress—it might be slow but remember to celebrate each step along the path as you become aware of what has already changed. Be grateful for that change. It is so easy to look at what is not yet there but try to focus on what is already there and be grateful for it.

I love to use a gratitude journal, especially one in which you write 3 to 5 things you are grateful for every day. Be grateful for the simple things in life, such as having a roof over your head, someone smiling at you today, or a nice conversation. Write it down and feel the gratitude. By doing this, you will notice that over time you are more focused on the things you have than the things you do not have. This attitude also applies to things we are not confident about. For example, I have a lot of cellulites on my upper legs, which I do not like. However, I am very grateful that these same legs bring me everywhere and help me to maintain my health by doing yoga and fitness. So instead of focusing on the cellulite, I focus on the gratitude. Additionally, business may not always be successful, but I am grateful for the small steps that help me to move in the right direction.

Another way I practice gratitude is by contributing to charitable causes. I'm a supporter of the B1G1 (Business for Good) organization. For every new client I acquire, I make a donation to one of their many projects. These contributions can fund various initiatives, such as providing meals for those in need, supporting rainforest conservation efforts, or planting trees. This practice of giving back not only benefits worthy causes but also fills me with a sense of gratitude and happiness.

My sister has been suffering from cancer for many years, and she is always grateful for what she is able to still experience. She cannot do any sports, but on the other hand, she is immensely grateful for the fact that she is living long enough to see her grandchildren grow up. Gratefulness helps us to have a positive outlook on life. Adapt an 'attitude of gratitude'.

BELIEVERS

So far, we have been doing most of the exercises alone and without the help or support of others. But in life, we need to surround ourselves with people that believe in us, that love us, and support us. Earlier, I mentioned that Tony Robbins claims, "you are the average of the five people you spend the most time with." When we surround ourselves with strong, high achievers with good character, we are more likely to become just like them. On the other hand, imagine how much of a negative influence people have on you who are talking negatively and do not believe in you or themselves.

Ask for help from a supportive network of people around you, when you need it; friends, colleagues, or family can encourage and uplift you. You can think of them as Your Believers. Having a strong support network can provide reassurance and perspective. If you feel you do not have these people in your environment yet, it may be worthwhile to join a network group of like-minded people. In return, be supportive to others, tell them you believe in them, tell them you appreciate them and are grateful that they are in your life.

Practice Self-Compassion and treat yourself with the same kindness and understanding you would offer a friend. Recognize that everyone makes mistakes and that these do not define your worth. I believe that we need others to help us be the best version of who we are.

When I returned to the office after having left my first husband, I noticed that we had a new colleague in the office, Frans.

We got to know each other; I found him attractive and liked him a lot. A short while after that, through work, I got invited to a tennis tournament in Antwerp, Belgium. The invite was for two people, and I asked Frans, to join me as I knew he loved tennis. He immediately said he would love to, however, only on the condition that he could drive, since he had just bought a brand-new Volkswagen Golf and was very proud of it. As we were close colleagues, I mentioned that we should go as colleagues and nothing more than that. He picked me up from my parents' house, where I was living again at the time, and I immediately regretted my remark about just being colleagues as he looked so handsome, and I was attracted to him.

The trip to Antwerp was fun, and we had loads to talk about. The tickets included dinner at a hotel, and we were transported by bus to the conference centre where the tennis tournament took place. Afterwards, we returned to the hotel to pick up the car. We drove out of the parking garage, and immediately a light started blinking on the dashboard. We stopped, and the manual clearly stated that we should not drive the car anymore. Returning to the hotel, we called road assistance. They said that the car needed to be towed away the next day and believe it or not, we had to stay at the hotel overnight! I remember thinking this is not happening, but it was, and we had to book a room for the night. The next morning, the car was towed away, and we had to remain in Antwerp the rest of the day as the car needed to be fixed. We called our employer and updated them on the situation in Antwerp. Eventually, the garage told us the car was fixed: only the light was broken. So, we had a big laugh, and even today, people think Frans planned it that way—I would agree if it were not for the fact that he is not that handy! When Frans dropped me back at my parents' house, we agreed we had a great time, but that was it. However, after a week, he phoned me in the evening and asked if I was as much in love with him as he was with me, and I confessed I was.

During our first date, I knew that if he would ask me to marry him that instant, I would say yes. It's weird how one can be very uncertain about some things, and yet this I knew 100% for sure. After a few years, we got married. As a result of Frans' continuous compliments and encouragement, I started feeling loved and confident and was able to develop myself further into the woman I am today. We have been married now for more than 33 years, and I am still happy with him. We sometimes think we know each other completely, but it's nice to explore the different sides of ourselves and each other in this safe environment of love.

When you are facing a challenge at work or in business and you believe you cannot do it, it can be extremely powerful if there is someone who tells you that you can actually do this. Someone who supports you, even when you fail, and helps you get up and try again. Have you ever seen an athlete without a coach or trainer achieve the best results? That is why I love mentoring. It helps to learn from others and maybe helps you to take shortcuts because then we do not have to make the same mistakes someone else already made or learn everything via our own trial and error process. Confidence in the workplace is not about knowing all the answers but about being willing to take risks, ask questions, and seek help when needed.

Years ago, I needed to hire an employee in my team. We interviewed a young man who was not very confident, but I truly believed in him. I had to convince both Human Resources and my line manager that we should hire him. I saw his potential, and after some mentoring, he flourished. Today, more than 20 years later, he has a managerial job in the same company, and he is doing well.

People telling us we can't do something can affect us in different ways. It depends on who we are and what's happening in our lives. For some people, like Anna, being told "you can't" makes them want to prove others wrong. When people said women couldn't be traders, it made Anna work harder to show she could. When I was struggling with my burnout, it initially hurt to hear that a coworker thought I could never return to my old job. But later, it pushed me to get better and return to work. However, not everyone reacts this way. For some people, hearing "you can't" can make them lose faith in themselves. It's important to know how these comments affect you personally. Sometimes they can make you try harder, and other times they can hold you back. Understanding your own reaction can help you use criticism to grow or protect yourself from letting it stop you from reaching your goals.

My best friends are my biggest fans and supporters. No matter what I do, they will tell me honestly what they think of it and help me get up and move on (and still love me) after I make mistakes. I hope for you that you have people in your life that do the same for you and if not, work on attracting people into your life who will provide you with this kind of positive support.

People that bring you down all the time are not the ones you want to spend most of your time with or work with. That does not mean they cannot give us feedback—on the contrary, feedback is good, but it should come with the best intentions. Feedback should not be designed to bring you down or to crash your confidence, but to support you to learn or grow your confidence. It's important to realize that if our life is a journey on a train, not everyone stays with us for the duration of the whole train ride. With some people, we have a nice interaction, but they leave at the next train station, while others will join us. Who do you want to share your journey with?

Exercise: Who Are Your Believers?

Write down who in your life has supported you and helped you grow, and who is not a supporter? Who do you want to continue hanging with (more) or less?

No matter how positive we are, there will be moments when we are triggered, and self-doubt comes up again. Know that it is very normal to have triggers in your life that may cause a temporary fallback into an old belief. And because you are now in the stage of being consciously incompetent, you are aware of it. It's important to realize that you are a 'student' who is studying to become proficient.

CHAPTER 6

Conscious Competence

In the previous chapter, I asked you to use the new sentences on the post-it notes and turn them into affirmations. Please do only one at a time, starting with the hardest one. After a few weeks, you will notice a shift when you repeat the new sentence. How does it feel to say out loud and where do you feel it in your body? Does this sentence make you happy? Confident, maybe? Can you take a mental picture of how it feels now?

What you have been doing is training the brain. When you repeatedly practice an activity or access a memory—in this case a limiting belief, saying e.g. "you are stupid"—neural networks (groups of neurons that fire together) create electrochemical pathways. If you spend years believing that what the voice said is true, these pathways are fired the moment something happens that can confirm that. Imagine a highway built between two points, A and B; so many thought-cars have driven the highway that the road is ingrained and familiar. During this exercise, you have been creating a new connection in the brain, which is a highway from A to C (the new belief) so you can understand why it takes time for the new road to be ingrained too. Knowing this makes it a lot easier to look at yourself in a compassionate way and realize that all you need to do is keep practicing and use the affirmation again. Bring compassion inward. The more often you use the affirmation, the sooner the 'road' will be ingrained, and the thought-car will run more smoothly. You will get there in time. Please be kind to yourself.

You are now conscious of the voices and have the tools (competence) to change them. However, it is not automatic yet. You will have to put in the effort and continue working on them. As with everything we want to learn and remember, it takes time and effort to learn. When you were a kid and learned to walk, you probably fell again and again. Fortunately, you persevered and eventually, you learned how to walk and how to run. Did you ever see a toddler giving up on learning how to walk? They try again and again, until the finally succeed. This is no different.

When you have practiced for several weeks and feel that you believe the affirmation, you can move on to the next sentence that is bothering you the most. Now you may wonder if you have to do this exercise with all the voices and sentences, but it is not necessary—once you gain more confidence and silence one or two of the voices, you will notice that the other ones are not that loud anymore.

Why? Because your energy has shifted. Quantum science has proven to us that everything is energy; that means that we are energy, and our thoughts, our emotions, our feelings, and nature are also energy. Can you imagine then that self-confidence is also a kind of energy and, when we gain more confidence, our energy therefore changes? When you feel more confident you may even start to stand straighter, your posture may change. You may want to change the way you look; you may want to wear bolder colours than you used to. By doing so, you will be radiating a different energy and feel different.

Ever had a situation in your life where everything seemed to go wrong? You get up in the morning and accidentally kick a glass of water beside your bed, spilling it all over the floor. You proceed to step under the shower and are startled that the water is cold, but you already put shampoo on your hair. You drive to work and there is an unexpected traffic jam. When you finally arrive at the office, you open your laptop, and it needs to run a scan first before you can begin work. From the moment things begin to go wrong, you may think that the day will not be so good, however the moment you start thinking this way, you let that belief lead the way for the rest of the day and it may come true through the energy you generate. Imagine the universe as a radio station: you generate a certain kind of frequency that is being 'heard' by similar energies and these energies are attracted by it. I am not saying that nothing bad will ever happen to you if you change the energy, of course, but by changing the way you deal with it, you can change the frequency and avoid attracting more misfortune.

When you gain more confidence: this will generate a frequency that attracts more confidence, and things will happen in your life to confirm that. At work, you may get chances you never believed were possible. But you need to take action. Only reading this book and waiting for things to happen will not be enough. Do the work and the exercises and realize that every now and then life will throw you a curveball. See that as a learning opportunity to become even better and more resilient.

Exercise: Confidence Journal

Start a confidence journal where you record daily instances of confident actions, no matter how small. Also, practice visualization techniques by spending a few minutes each day picturing yourself handling challenging situations with confidence.

When I was around 15 years old, I went on holiday with my parents. My father was not the best driver in the world and my mother was always afraid when she was in the car with him. During this 1200-kilometer trip, my mother was sitting in the back, extremely tense, and she held on tightly to the seatbelt of the front seat during the whole trip. After we had travelled about 1175 km, we had a car crash, and we were all badly hurt. This wasn't due to my father's driving, but due to the other driver, but it was quite a shock for all of us.

When I turned 18 and was allowed to drive, I took lessons, but I was so scared and nervous that I probably drove the driving instructor completely nuts and sometimes he lost his patience. It goes without saying that I was extremely insecure when driving; it took many lessons and 4 exams before I passed. And, even when I received my driving license, I still had to become proficient by gaining more experience. I can tell you that quite often I was shaking in the car when I had to drive a longer distance, but I kept doing it and practicing until one day I was not nervous anymore and was able to simply get in the car and drive.

When you start a new job, you need to learn new and different things, e.g., new systems, processes, the culture. During your onboarding (and I hope you have one), you are meeting new colleagues and learning from them or often nowadays from online learning programs. You might experience an overwhelming feeling and think this is so much to learn, and that new system is so complicated to use. You may even wonder if you will ever be able to learn this. But a few months later and many hours of using the system, you have become quite familiar with it, and you won't find it difficult anymore. You have gained confidence while using the system. Do you recall a moment where you found learning something was very difficult, but eventually, that same thing seemed easy after a while?

This experience reminds me of Carol Dweck's work. Dweck is a renowned psychologist and professor at Stanford University, known for her research on mindset. She explains that believing your qualities can be developed fosters resilience and a love of learning, essential for great accomplishment. Her concept of the growth mindset is pivotal in transforming insecurity into confidence. In my case with driving, adopting a growth mindset helped me persist through the challenges, believing that I could improve with practice and effort, ultimately leading to my increased confidence behind the wheel.

So, now you are consciously competent! And that's the end of the lessons, right? Well, not quite.

Sometimes there are 'triggers' that make you forget your new competence. Though driving had become something automatic for me after years of practice, one day while driving in bad weather on a large bridge, one of my tyres burst while I was going more than 100 kilometres an hour. Naturally, I panicked. The car was out of control. I remembered that when your tyres burst you should not brake, so I released the gas and put my car into another gear, and by doing so I was able to steer the car to the side without hitting someone else. There I was on the side of the road, shaking with fear. Fortunately, help was on its way. They told me I had to bring my car to the nearest garage which was only 5 kilometres away. For a moment, I thought: "I do not dare to do that, I do not want to" and then my old 'belief and fear' about driving kicked in. But I also realized that I had safely stopped the car, proving that I could manage even in extreme situations, which gave me back enough confidence to drive to the garage.

After that incident, I was less secure behind the wheel for a while, but I had learned how to talk to myself and regain my confidence. Soon, I forgot all about that incident. I had the tools to consciously be competent again.

Step 5: Mind Your Power State

Remember in chapter 3 that you decided on your power-word? Remember what yours is? As mentioned, mine is PARAGLIDING. When something daunting or challenging comes my way and I need some extra courage, confidence, and power, I use the power-word: PARAGLIDING. However, I am not only using this word, but using my body to feel it, too.

When you think about that one thing that gave you courage and made you feel strong and is your power-word, I would like you to *feel* where in your body you can feel this. Maybe in your heart area, maybe in your belly—it can be anywhere. Feel it. Now, what kind of physical movement would be suitable to help you remember this specific feeling? Let us call that a power-move. For me, it is swinging my arms back and forth with strength. What is your power move?

One of my clients makes his hands into fists and powerfully pushes his elbows up and down. Feel what yours is. Try a few positions out to see what makes you feel strong and powerful.

Now make that move at least 10 times while saying the power word. For me, this would mean saying "PARAGLIDING" and making a forward move with one arm, with my hand clenched into a fist, as if I am boxing.

This way, we make a connection between the movement and the feeling of power, so that whenever you need it and use it again, you will feel stronger and more confident. This creates a pathway in your brain—the highway we talked about earlier in this chapter.

You may wonder if the confidence you gained by now will remain forever. If only it were that simple! Life is unpredictable, and as much as we like to, we cannot control it. First, we need to realize that we are only in control of some smaller things, but there are plenty of things we cannot control. Ever heard of Steven Covey and his work "The 7 Habits of Highly Effective People"? In this book, he introduces the concept of the Circle of Influence to help you focus on what you can control and influence, rather than expending energy on things outside your control. He divides our concerns into two circles: the Circle of Concern and the Circle of Influence.

The Circle of Concern includes everything we care about but do not have direct control over. This could include global issues like climate change, political events, or even the behaviour of other people of what others thing of us. Within the larger Circle of Concern lies the Circle of Influence, which includes all the areas where we can directly impact outcomes. This includes our attitudes, behaviours, and choices, such as what we eat. By concentrating on our Circle of Influence, we can proactively work towards change and improvement in areas where our actions make a difference.

Can you imagine how focusing on the Circle of Concern can make you worry about things you have far less influence and control over? This may lead to a feeling of being powerless and can result in frustration and a sense of failure, as we fixate on problems beyond our control. It can significantly impact our confidence and self-worth.

One of my clients suffers from this a lot. Whenever she watches the news, she feels terrible and lies awake, wanting to change everything she cannot control. It affects her so much that she feels powerless and unworthy.

On the other hand, when we focus on our Circle of Influence, we invest our time and energy in areas where we can effect change. This proactive focus enhances our sense of control and empowers us to make meaningful contributions to our goals and the world around us. And as such, it can increase our self-confidence.

How would this work for your business/work?

Below are several examples:

Conflict with colleagues: Let's assume you and your co-worker do not get along. Rather than focusing on the behaviour of that colleague, focus on what you do and how you may be able to have a better relationship. This is exactly what I did with the colleague from the legal department. I could not control her response, but I could control mine, and this resulted in a different relationship. And if your colleague is unpleasant and the situation cannot be helped, then you may decide to look for opportunities at another company or department.

Leadership: Good leaders focus on their team's mood, growth, and work instead of just worrying about outside business conditions. This helps create a stronger, more motivated team. We know that to make customers happier, we need to make employees happier first. When workers enjoy their jobs more, customers end up more satisfied too.

With regards to your personal life: those who prioritize their health, learning, and relationships rather than external validation or uncontrollable events often experience greater satisfaction and well-being. You do not have to wait for others or need the appreciation of someone else.

In conclusion, by focusing on what we can influence, we not only maximize our effectiveness but also cultivate a life with less worry, more confidence, and fulfilment.

"If you want to change the world, first change yourself".

Triggers

Congratulations, you have already done a lot of reading and work. However, you may realize that just when you think: "Now I have all the confidence I need," something might happen that temporarily sets you back. Do you have to start all over again? No, fortunately not. Let us have a look at what might set you back.

My friend Loubna, who is now very confident and loves herself a lot, told me that even today, sometimes when people do not like her and express that, it brings her out of balance, and the self-doubt miraculously surfaces again. What to do then? Well, what she does, is look at the situation from a helicopter perspective—zooming out to see the bigger picture. She observes what happened and starts 'grounding' herself in the body. Then she asks questions of herself to help herself realize that the comment may be a projection of the other person rather than a problem with her, and if not, that is okay too. You do not have to be loved and liked by everyone; there are 8 billion people on the planet, and there are plenty out there that do like you. Loubna reminds herself that it is okay; she loves herself with all her flaws and strengths and knows she is worthy. The way she recovers is a great example of resilience, and an inspiration to us all.

Now we all have triggers. What are yours? Or maybe even better: who are yours? Is there a pattern? Observe yourself when something brings you out of balance. What happened? Ask yourself why it triggered you. In my own experience, family members can trigger things inside you. Also, when the pressure is on and there are many things to do at the same time, we may get triggered. You may have a deadline at work or perhaps you are required to do several new things that you are not skilled in yet.

When I was asked to teach a course in a subject, I was not yet an expert in, I felt triggered. It made me wonder, "What if someone is an expert and they ask a question I do not know? What if they will notice that I do not know everything about this area? What if, etc. etc.?" Eventually, I told myself, "You know what? They asked me to give a lecture in this area. I still have time to get my knowledge up to speed, and because they believed I was suitable, I was asked to do this." I had promised myself some time ago that even if something is out of my comfort zone, I will say yes to it. And so, I did. Indeed, there were some subject matter experts in the classroom, but unlike me, they did not have the experience in that area at work, only from books, and I realized that was exactly the reason I had been asked to give those lectures.

What I was suffering from was a clear example of something called "Imposter Syndrome."

The Imposter Syndrome

Imposter syndrome is a common issue where individuals doubt their abilities despite clear evidence of their success. Do you know that feeling when you know you are good at something, but when you are asked to use that knowledge/skill, suddenly you hear the voice in your head saying, "What if they find out I am not so good at this? What if they think I am a fraud? What if... what if...?" What does this voice say to you when you are triggered? According to a 2019 study published in the International Journal of Behavioral Science, 70% of high-achieving individuals experience imposter syndrome at some point in their careers. This feeling of inadequacy and self-doubt is experienced particularly among women, who often face more triggers and societal pressure. As someone who has coached many women, I know firsthand the impact of imposter syndrome. Women are the ones most likely to undermine their own value and progress. We can be our worst enemy and often hold ourselves back from pursuing goals. To counteract this, it's crucial to acknowledge your strengths—both personally and professionally—especially when navigating change management. And also, to support other women in doing so.

TIP 1:

Naming these feelings can be the first step to overcoming them. If we ignore them, they will continue to pop up like an unwanted pimple.

Judith, who is now a director in trading for a big bank, still suffers from imposter syndrome every now and then. When she needs to present for an audience, and the same type of men are there that told her she—as a woman—would never succeed in trading (her trigger), imposter syndrome hits her hard. However, she only allows it for a short moment. She has learned how to feel confident again and takes the stage with pride to show everyone how good she is at what she does.

TIP 2:

You may want to make a list of your accomplishments so that you can have a look when the imposter comes and visits you. Imagine you are showing the list to the imposter. Maybe you will even ask, "So, what have you, imposter, accomplished so far aside from creating doubt and low self-esteem? Thank you for warning me, but the evidence is here. See what I have accomplished so far."

Loubna has the same feeling as Judith before walking onto a big stage. She wonders why she ever said yes to this, and then she does it anyway. The imposter is simply that—an imposter in your head. It is telling lies, so reply by saying thank you but no, we are not listening anymore to those lies. We know our worth and that we are enough.

TIP 3:

Remember to take one small step at a time to grow. Very few have gone up the ladder with giant steps. Taking small steps which make your circle of comfort a little bit bigger each time will help you gain confidence for the next step and the next and the next. When you are first starting to speak up at work, I would not advise trying to take on a big stage; speak up in your department meeting first and take it from there.

Resilience

Resilience is the ability to bounce back from setbacks, adapt to change, and keep going in the face of adversity. It's not just about surviving tough times but thriving despite them. In a world where challenges are inevitable, resilience is crucial for personal and professional success. Here's how you can build resilience and implement solutions to alleviate stress.

In other words: when we are in pieces (or triggered), we are vulnerable, but when we carefully glue all the pieces together and see what we can learn from what happened, we can see the gold and rise stronger and more beautiful. That, for me, is resilience. In Japan, there is the beautiful art of Kintsugi. This practice not only fixes the broken object but also highlights and celebrates its cracks and repairs, often making the piece more beautiful and unique than it was before. Kintsugi is often seen as a metaphor for embracing flaws and imperfections, seeing beauty in the scars and history of an object or even a person.

Becoming more resilient is like training a muscle. It will not grow overnight, but after a lot of practice, it becomes easier and goes a lot quicker.

How can you become more resilient? Look at what you have already done and overcome in your life. You have grown from a baby to an adult—that by itself is amazing when we think about it. Look back and remember where you come from and where you are now. Whatever you are facing in this moment, you will get through it.

My sister has been suffering from different types of cancer for more than 30 years now. There have been many moments when we thought she would not live another year and yet she is still there. Her resilience is really amazing. She has a lot of pain every day and yet always has a good mood and enjoys all the small things in life. Even when she has a bad message from the doctors, she seems to recuperate within a short time. In that sense, she is for me an amazing example of resilience and of how: 'Life isn't about waiting for the storm to pass... It's about learning to dance in the rain.' Witnessing her unwavering spirit has profoundly shaped my own approach to life's challenges. When I face obstacles, I often think of my sister and find strength in her example, reminding myself that if she can find joy amidst such adversity, I too can face my struggles with grace and determination.

People often say about successful entrepreneurs that they are the ones who have fallen and gotten up one more time. This highlights the resilience and perseverance of entrepreneurs, emphasizing that setbacks are just part of the journey toward success.

My first business was in fashion. Having studied Fashion Design in London, I wanted to start my own business and sell limited editions of a collection for women that made them feel more confident. The fabrics were all sourced from sustainable suppliers. The production took place in the Netherlands at a company that paid their workers good wages and had great working conditions. All this resulted in a high price tag. Soon after my launch a famous Dutch entrepreneur decided to open 5 luxury department stores in the Netherlands, and she wanted to buy my whole collection, but under consignment, which means you only get paid when they sell something. Unfortunately, the luxury department stores went bankrupt within a year and though I was able to get most of my products back, there were missing sizes, and I could not sell it to other retailers anymore. I tried and tried but to no avail. Every time I walked past these clothes, it reminded me of what happened and how I failed. My former director, who is also a friend, said to me, "Karina, look at this differently. See this as an expensive course you took and from which you learnt a lot".

This made me wonder why I started this business, and I realized that I wanted to support women to feel more confident. I did not need to do this through clothes, although it's true clothes that can help you to feel more confident but is not the full solution. This eventually led me where I am today. I don't regret any of it; it was indeed an expensive but very useful learning experience. Currently, I have a successful business and enjoy what I am doing much more than in my former business. In the end, it was all in my favour. Had I not started my fashion business, I may not have had the business I currently have.

Did my disappointment of failing leave overnight? Certainly not, but I learned a lot from my setback and started all over again.

Self-care

These days, there are many ways to increase your resilience. It is crucial to take care of yourself. Before you start your day: feel your body. Are there places that feel contracted and tight? Maybe they even hurt? Pay attention and breathe. Personally, I have been practicing heart coherence techniques for years. Heart coherence is a measurable state of physiological synchronization between the heart, brain, and autonomic nervous system. It's characterized by a smooth, sine-wave-like pattern in heart rate variability. Achieving coherence involves learning to generate and sustain positive emotions like care, appreciation, and compassion, which can be facilitated through specific breathing techniques. When in a coherent state, the body's systems operate more efficiently, potentially leading to improved emotional stability, cognitive function, and stress resilience. Heart coherence practices aim to calm the nervous system, reduce the impact of stress reactions, and enhance decision-making capabilities. As a heart coherence coach, I've guided many individuals in developing these skills to boost their overall resilience. The breathing techniques used are simple yet powerful, and their effects have been documented in numerous scientific studies, particularly by organizations like the HeartMath Institute.

Our brain is bombarded with 11.2 million bits of information every single second, which determines if we are safe or unsafe. Stress makes us feel unsafe. Back when humans were hunters, we sometimes had to run away from a predatory wild animal, and the stress hormones helped us to survive. Nowadays, there are not many wild animals anymore, though we seem to have created our own. In a culture of constant productivity, we do not know how to relax anymore. Through breathing exercises, we can calm the mind and reconnect with ourselves and release stress. This is so important because otherwise, the hormones that are related to stress will keep building up in our body. Through coherent breathing, we tell the body: you are safe, and we start producing different (healthier) hormones. That way we increase our resilience. If you want to know more about this research, see . For me and many others this works. What works for you is something you need to find out. Maybe it is walking in nature, singing, running, whatever. As long as you experience safety, you will calm down, which helps to build resilience.

Now you may think that sounds nice, but I do not have the time. I challenge you to think instead that the busier you are, the more important it is to take care of yourself. Make the time. Get up 30 minutes earlier, and if you have small kids, you may want to use the last 30 minutes before you sleep to work on self-care.

TIP 4:

How can you practice this at work?

- Breathe deep in and out for 10 times at least three times a day.

- Have a mentor, someone who will help you to overcome difficulties at work and has your best interest at heart.

- Work on your work/life integration: find out what feels best for you. When you are already stressed because you are running a family and a company and/or a demanding job, it's easy to see why you might be triggered much quicker. And rather than wanting to work on your work/life balance, I advise you to work on bringing harmony into your life. If that means you can work 4 days a week 9 hours and have a day off, go for it.

These are only a few examples, there are many more. What do you do to increase your resilience? Make a list of things that make you feel relaxed and that you love to do.

Aside from many positive effects: when you are resilient it is easier and quicker to bounce back after setbacks and triggers.

"It is not stress that causes a burnout, it is a lack of recovery that causes a burnout."

From experience I can tell you: if something brings your confidence down, it is a burnout. It's important to work on your mental well-being every single day.

I told you earlier that I made myself a promise to say yes to new things. I won't deny that this promise can be very uncomfortable at times. However, I've learned to ask myself: "What's the worst that could happen if I do this? Really, what's the worst?"

For example, when writing this book, I ask myself: "What's the worst that could happen? People might not like me or the book. Or they might not hire me as a keynote speaker." This helps me realize that it's not the end of the world, and I'll survive whatever happens. And what if I think differently? What if people like my book and I am hired as a keynote speaker?

Look at things from a wider perspective. Take a helicopter view by zooming out and seeing the bigger picture of your life and compare its relevance to the bigger things that are going on in the world.

According to Dr. Kristin Neff, practicing self-compassion can significantly reduce anxiety and depression while boosting overall well-being. She says: "Whenever I notice something about myself, I don't like, or whenever something goes wrong in my life, I silently repeat the following phrases: This is a moment of suffering. Suffering is part of life. May I be kind to myself in this moment. May I give myself the compassion I need." Her research shows that self-compassion helps individuals manage stress and promotes a positive mindset. By integrating self-compassion into daily routines, we can cultivate a healthier relationship with ourselves and enhance our emotional resilience.

Trust yourself and trust that the Universe has got your back. Things happen in your life and what if they happen FOR you instead of happening TO you? Looking from this perspective, we realize that no matter how bad a situation is, there is always something we can learn from it.

Whatever it is:

"This too shall pass."

Chapter 7
Unconscious Competence

"The best and most beautiful things in the world cannot be seen or even touched. They must be felt with the heart."

Hellen Keller

Congratulations, we are now in the final chapter of the book, and you have already gained awareness and tools on how to improve your confidence. Now, let us take this a step further and see how you can unconditionally love yourself. Realize that Love is a verb, so that means even though you may feel that you are unconditionally loving yourself, you still need to nurture and embed that.

Self-love is our base, the rock you can always come back to. It has been there all your life; you have simply wrapped it up in so many voices and beliefs that you could not see it has been there all along. Now it is time to fully embrace it. You may wonder why we did not start this book with self-love in that case, but if you are not used to practicing self-love, you first need to have confidence. With confidence comes the courage to love yourself unconditionally.

Step 6: Mind your Self-Love

Do you have the courage to stand up and look at yourself in the mirror and say, "I love you"? If so, can you really feel the love you have for yourself?

Self-love is a solid rock foundation you can always come back to; it is unconditional, not depending on others or what you do or have done, or how you look, what your job title is, or how much money or prestige you earn. When you truly love yourself, you will notice that no wind, no storm, no rain can harm it.

Confidence is much thinner and easier to bruise; that is why we get triggered and often need to recuperate again. If we have confidence but no self-love, we might become like the Hungry Caterpillar in the famous children's story. Just as the caterpillar eats and eats, never feeling satisfied, we might constantly seek praise and validation from others, never feeling truly confident or content. However, the caterpillar's transformation into a beautiful butterfly can represent our own journey. By developing self-love - our cocoon of inner strength - we can emerge as our true selves, no longer hungry for external validation. Self-love is the key to becoming your own magnificent butterfly, confident and self-assured from within.

If you do not feel comfortable saying that you love yourself, let us see how you can get there or, if you can say it, let's work on ways you can even love yourself more.

Exercise: What Do You Love About Yourself

Write three things you love about yourself each day and read them aloud every morning.

Forgiveness

One of the areas that is important is to forgive. Is there something in your life or maybe someone you have a grudge against? Or are there things in your life that you regret doing?

Forgiving others or yourself does not mean you forget or approve what they or you have done, but simply that you forgive it. Holding a grudge, anger, or frustration towards someone or you will actually hold you back. Therefore, forgiving is something you do for yourself.

Forgiveness has been a crucial part of my transformation. There was indeed much to forgive. Reflecting on my youth, I had to learn how to forgive my father, whose tantrums and aggressive behaviour frightened me. I've come to understand that, in his own way, he did the best he could. Despite his shortcomings, I know he loved my mother, sister, and me.

I am a firm believer that there is a lesson in everything we go through, and I found that his way of upbringing also made my sister and me able to deal with setbacks and how to persevere. As a result, we know how to be strong.

There are many beautiful meditations (e.g., the 6-phase meditation from Vishen Lakhiani) that can help you to forgive. The most important thing to remember is that you forgive for yourself. If we hold on to what happened and feel hatred, resentment, etc., then that negative energy is holding us in its power. Do you want what happened to you or the one that did this to you to have that power over you and your current life? I'm sure you don't, and that is why we forgive. Sometimes we get stuck in what happened long ago and let it still influencing or maybe even ruining our lives in the present. When we forgive, we let go of that part and move on with our lives. Please work on forgiveness, give yourself the gift to forgive and move on. Love yourself enough to move on.

Do not let your past be your present

If you hold on to the past and keep repeating what happened, this makes an imprint in your brain, like the highway we talked about earlier in this book. Our body does not know the difference between reality and the past. If you relive the past continuously, your body will feel as if the experience is still going on, and that will release the same kind of stress, hormones, anger, disappointment, etc., as if it had just happened moments ago. To stop this, we need to forgive. Stop being a victim and know that no matter what happened, you can choose how what happened will affect your life going forward.

"Yesterday is history, Tomorrow is a mystery.
Today is a gift, that is why we call it Present."
Master Oogway (from the movie Kung Fu Panda)

Another effective way on the path to forgiveness is Ho'oponopono: The Hawaiian Art of Forgiveness. The Ho'oponopono practice involves four key phrases:
• I'm sorry.
• Please forgive me.
• Thank you.
• I love you.
These phrases are used to facilitate healing and forgiveness, promoting peace and harmony within oneself and with others. To fully love ourselves, we should not feel hate.

Quantum science has shown that emotions have different energetic qualities. Dr. David R. Hawkins, in his book "Power vs. Force," introduced a scale of consciousness that ranks emotional states from lower to higher levels. This scale, while not based on traditional scientific measurements of frequency, suggests that emotions like fear, shame, guilt, and anger are associated with lower levels of consciousness, whereas emotions like love, joy, peace, and compassion are associated with higher levels. Understanding this scale can help you recognize the importance of cultivating higher-consciousness emotions for personal and professional growth. As such, our mood is transmitting a frequency too. Though you may not actually see this visually, you can feel and sense it.

Do you know that feeling when you enter a room with people, you immediately sense whom to stay away from and who you are attracted to? Now, if we consider ourselves a transmission pole through which all those frequencies are broadcasted, can you imagine that if we broadcast vibrations, others pick this up? This is the case for lower and higher vibrations. And when we hold anger or shame, these frequencies are in the way of achieving the higher vibrations of joy, love, and peace. That is why we do not want to be stuck in limited beliefs and need to forgive. This will clear the path to enter higher vibrations and to be able to feel love for ourselves.

Embodiment

During a seminar with Tony Robbins, I had a big breakthrough. There in London, together with 12,000 people, I got rid of some of the most stubborn limited beliefs I had been holding on to for way too long. And yet, a few weeks after the seminar, I still felt something was missing. It was not until I read the work of Dr. Joe

Dispenza and then the work of Dr. Sue Morter that I realized the missing part was 'embodiment'. We can do amazing things with our mind. However, to fully transform, we need to reconnect the mind with the body and soul.

My burnout made me realize that I was living too much in my head and had lost the connection to my body. Some people even do not know how to feel or cannot identify what they feel anymore. What about you?

Since my recovery from burnout, I do fitness and yoga several times a week and re-learned how to relax, which was a great lesson and a blessing in disguise. It could have been much worse, had I not learned to listen to my body. In the end, it was all in my favour, as it also was the start of attending many courses and reading books about Personal Development. I promised myself I would never let myself burn out again. It made me realize that until that moment, I had lived in a way where things would just happen to me, and I had the feeling that I had no control over my own journey. I underwent life instead of living life.

Are you truly living your life? When you listen to what the negative voices in your head say, would you consider them to be friends? I bet that in most cases your answer is no. If a friend would say these same unhelpful things to you, would you still be friends? Why on earth would you continue to be friends with someone who nags you all the time? In that sense, you are your own enemy. No wonder you do not love yourself. But no longer—now it's time to forgive yourself; until today, you did not know better.

> *"Love yourself, be clear on how you want to be*
> *treated. Know your worth always."*
>
> Maryam Hasnaa

Like so many others, I was not brought up in a way that taught me to love myself. Instead, I used to believe that I should love other people before loving myself, and that self-love was selfish. But I know now that the greatest gift you can give to others is to love yourself. How can you even truly love someone else if you do not love yourself?

It reminds me of being in a plane, when the safety instructions tell you that in case of an emergency you need to put on your own oxygen mask first before taking care of others. That is how it works with self-love too. When you love yourself, you are able to love others more, to have more compassion, and as a result, you will enter into better relationships with others. And because of this ripple effect, others will have more compassion for you in turn, and eventually, we all benefit from this. So even if you find it difficult to do this for yourself: do it for the greater good. It will be better for the planet.

In the previous chapters, you have turned limited beliefs into positive affirmations, you have practiced gratitude and got back or more in touch with how and what you feel. Now can you tell yourself that you love yourself? And mean it? If you can—congratulations!

If not, practice saying you love yourself in the mirror every day. For some people this may feel very uncomfortable, since some people associate self-love with narcissism or arrogance. You may even feel resentment about the exercise.

Narcissism

Narcissism is a personality trait defined on Dictionary.com as "a person who is overly self-involved, and often vain and selfish" as well as being clinically specific. A narcissist, from a psychiatric perspective, is a person suffering from narcissistic personality disorder (NPD), a formal diagnosis for someone comprising "a pervasive pattern of grandiosity (in fantasy or behaviour), need for admiration and lack of empathy." According to Dr. David M. Reiss, "Narcissism has been around as long as humanity has been around — and has been recognized for that long and a true narcissist is concerned ONLY with themselves and their needs".

Some of the traits of a narcissist are:

- Self-concern, self-centeredness and self-consciousness that is disproportionate.

- Extreme sensitivity to negative feedback or criticism.

- Significant need for approval from others due to inadequacies that are real or imagined.

- Difficulties within most relationships.

- Intolerance for imperfections in others.

- Often idealize others that represent perfection followed by devaluing that very person when they are perceived to have failed them.

- Preoccupation with outward appearance, beauty, wealth, fame, success over morals, virtue or even integrity.

- Poor emotional regulation, aggressive impulses, psychologically fragile Vain, self-righteous and prideful.

- Lack remorse, compassion, empathy for others.

We all have some narcissistic qualities, as the trait spans a spectrum. There is however a radical difference between having narcissistic qualities (e.g., being self-centred) and being a true narcissist. You may consider this: if you are worried that you might be a narcissist, you probably are not one. Narcissists generally lack the kind of empathetic self-reflection that might make them wonder if they have a personality disorder.

Have you ever worked with a narcissist? I have, and it was extremely difficult. Everyone was complaining about how Pierre treated others. When confronting him with this, he told me that it was not his behaviour but the incompetence of everyone around him that caused the issues. Because they feared retaliation, no one in the department dared to make a formal complaint against him. However, one day a supplier called me and said that Pierre's attitude had led to one of the salespeople crying. Pierre claimed the salesperson only cried because he was incompetent. I had a very serious conversation with Pierre (after, of course, checking all the facts with the supplier and others who had witnessed the situation). After this conversation, I sent him an email summarizing everything we had discussed. As soon as he received the email, he called me and accused me of writing down lies, despite my careful notetaking during our conversation. I told him that if he felt that way, he should email back with his objections, as this email would also go to Human Resources. He did not respond, but following a restructuring of the company, there was no longer a job for him. Unsurprisingly, Pierre blamed the company for his layoff rather than acknowledging any fault on his part. It should be clear that he lacked the ability to self-reflect.

"Confidence isn't thinking you are better than everyone else; it's realizing that you have no reason to compare yourself to anyone else."

Maryam Hasnaa

Arrogance

Maybe you connect self-love and confidence to arrogance, but there is a clear distinction. Arrogance often manifests as a superiority complex, where individuals feel and act as though they are better than others. This attitude is usually accompanied by a lack of empathy, as arrogant people tend to disregard others' feelings and perspectives. Whereas self-love is rooted in self-acceptance, arrogance is often driven by a deep-seated insecurity and a constant need for external validation. Arrogant individuals are highly competitive, focusing on being the best and proving others wrong, rather than on personal development. Consequently, they frequently dismiss the contributions and ideas of others as unworthy.

Self-love involves embracing oneself with all strengths and weaknesses, fostering empathy and compassion for yourself and others. Unlike arrogance, self-love is derived from intrinsic validation; it's about recognizing your worth without needing constant approval from others. This genuine confidence fuels personal growth and improvement, not at the expense of others, but in harmony with them. People who practice self-love respect others, valuing their opinions and contributions, which nurtures positive and respectful relationships. You fully accept yourselves, know your strengths and weaknesses, and are both aware and okay with them.

Now that we have taken the belief that self-love and narcissism are the same out of the way, is there something else holding you back when you say you love yourself?

Can you think about something or someone that you love? If you can, please close your eyes for a moment and locate the place in your body where this love originates. Maybe you do not feel anything yet; just imagine it for now. Or maybe you can think about a situation where you felt loved or had a deep love for someone or something—it can be a family member, a friend, or maybe a pet or a hobby you love to do. Can you feel it now? Take a mental picture of how that feels and really feel it. Now imagine that this is how it feels to love yourself; how is that and how does it feel? Hopefully, it feels good, and you would like to practice this feeling as often as possible. Put a post-it note on the mirror stating: 'I love myself' and say it as often as you can. Don't just say it but feel and believe it.

Over time it will be easier to say that to yourself and you will grant yourself the self-love you deserve and need.

Step 7: Mind your Values

Throughout the book, you discovered what kind of voices are talking to you, and you became aware of the negative self-talk. Because of all the noise that is going on inside our heads most of the time, we cannot hear what our body and heart is telling. That is why we needed to become aware of the voices and reverse them into positive talk, so that there will be more room for love. Then there will also be room to tap into our intuition.

To create a permanent change, we have to take a look at what drives us. What do you find important? What makes you get out of bed in the morning? What motivates you to make changes in your life? And for that, we need to find out what our values are.

Below there is a list of core values (but there are more, and you can find ample tests to find out your values online).

Core Values

Authenticity

Achievement

Adventure

Authority

Autonomy

Balance

Beauty

Boldness

Compassion

Challenge

Citizenship

Community

Competency

Contribution

Creativity

Curiosity

Determination

Fairness

Faith

Fame

Friendships

Fun

Growth

Happiness

Honesty

Humour

Influence

Inner Harmony

Justice

Kindness

Knowledge

Leadership

Learning

Love

Loyalty

Meaningful Work

Openness

Optimism

Peace

Pleasure

Poise

Popularity

Recognition

Religion

Reputation

Respect

Responsibility

Security

Self-Respect

Service

Spirituality

Stability

Success

Status

Transparency

Trustworthiness

Wealth

Wisdom

Exercise: Rank Your Values

Make a top 10 and rank them in order of importance. Now from the 10, choose the three most important ones and rank them too. This will give you insights into what you value over something else. For example, my top 3 values are:

1. Authenticity

2. Transparency

3. Trustworthiness

Please go to https://www.confidenceatwork.nl/resources/ to download the worksheet.

Simon Sinek stresses that knowing your 'why'—your core values—drives leadership and inspires others, highlighting the significance of values in personal and professional life. As Sinek famously puts it, "People don't buy what you do; they buy why you do it. And what you do simply proves what you believe." This underscores the importance of understanding and living by your values to lead effectively and authentically. Our values impact our decisions, as the story below shows.

Years ago, I worked as the head of procurement (buying) in an international company, and we had to choose a vendor for a large project. A request for proposal was made, and several suppliers made a proposal. One supplier was the favourite, and yet, something did not seem right to me. After having worked in procurement for many years, I knew I had the experience and knowledge and should not neglect that feeling. And as trustworthiness is in the top 3 of my values, for me, this is more important than, for example, social acceptance. Everyone involved in the process was in favour of this vendor. So, what to do? I had a good relationship with the financial director and decided to talk to him. I explained my worries to him and told him that my intuition told me something was off and the offer from this vendor was not right. He looked at me and said he had full trust and if my intuition was that strong, we should not choose that vendor. I was surprised by his response and was happy that he had so much faith in me and in my gut feeling. Eventually, we chose another supplier, and later we found out that indeed the other supplier's offer was neither trustworthy nor accurate.

Looking back, I notice that I had confidence in my skills and my intuition, and that gave me the courage to speak up to the financial director. What would have happened if I had simply accepted the majority opinion? Well, I would have been very unhappy afterward if I had found out that my intuition was right, but I had not followed it. Additionally, the company I worked for would have lost hundreds of thousands of Euros.

Remember my friend, the weightlifter? She could have won the Olympic games if she had ignored her own values. Her most important one was her health. If she had given in to what people expected her to do, she would have jeopardized her health. But she did not. Her values were even more important than winning the Olympic games.

How do your values influence your actions at work? It is equally important to understand how others' values influence their actions. For example, if a line manager values boldness above all else, he may often make bold statements, which might not sit well with team members who prioritize stability. This difference in values can cause friction and impact the team atmosphere.

When working in a team, it is useful to identify and understand the values that each team member holds dear. Additionally, remember that these values extend beyond the workplace and influence your personal life as well.

Self-acceptance

How can you love yourself when you do not accept yourself the way you are without judgment or resistance? Fortunately, by now, you have gained confidence and hopefully let go of some limited beliefs. But you may still have areas in your life you are not content with accepting them. It is okay not to be perfect. Even the most beautiful or 'perfect' people have flaws; we all do. So let us accept that we are all *Perfectly Imperfect*. Celebrate your uniqueness!

Have you heard of Nick Vujicic? Nick was born without limbs. Despite his physical limitations, his courage and tenacity for life have caused him to become one of the biggest motivational speakers in the world, known as an expert on resilience and reframing challenges. He is married and has 4 kids.

Rather than feeling like a victim for not having arms or legs, he is celebrating his uniqueness with lots and lots of love and helping others to do so as well. He can do things no one thought was possible. Others might perceive his disability as a 'flaw,' but instead it's a gift that strengthens him, and through using his talents he has helped millions of people.

'If you always do what you always did, you will always get what you always got.'

Albert Einstein

The biggest innovations come from thinking and doing differently, so celebrate your uniqueness and your gifts. When I was offered a job interview for a procurement position on an interim basis at a big pharmaceutical company, I was initially reluctant because the commute was long and traffic was always an issue. Despite my hesitation, I went for the interview and had a pleasant conversation with the line manager. During the interview, he mentioned that he had already found a suitable candidate but agreed to meet with me because the hiring company insisted. He noticed that my approach to procurement was different and ended up offering me the job, realizing he needed someone with a fresh perspective. I accepted the position and ended up staying there for more than five years.

Embrace your authenticity. Once you have enough confidence, you will know what your strengths and weaknesses are. And that is okay; accept that, embrace it, and love it.

If love were a blanket, you could wrap yourself with it, feel the warmth and gentleness, fully emerge, become the blanket, and become love. Picture how that would feel. Give yourself a hug. Be nice to yourself. Have compassion.

Vulnerability

"Vulnerability is not about winning or losing.
It's having the courage to show up even when
you can't control the outcome".

Brené Brown

Self-love allows for vulnerability and openness without fear of rejection or judgment. Years ago, I was managing a team in a multinational company, and one man in my team was rather vocally aggressive, and I – as his line manager – honestly feared him. In addition, he was not functioning well, so I had to have some tough conversations with him that would keep me awake at night. I feared him because he reminded me of my father, and his outbursts triggered this feeling inside me. After trying all kinds of ways to have a normal conversation with him, one day I decided to be vulnerable. Of course, that scared me. I was afraid he would use this vulnerability against me, but I realized I had nothing to lose.

I told him that my father had a similar way of communicating and his behaviour upset me. That conversation was a turning point. He had no idea his behaviour affected me like that, and we agreed on a codeword. Whenever he would cross my boundaries, I would mention the codeword. And you know what it was? CALIMERO—you may be familiar with the cartoon of the little duckling with an eggshell on his head.

By being extremely vulnerable as his line manager, we ended up having a solid work relationship. Believe it or not, vulnerability can be your superpower too.

To be a good leader (both for business and for your own life), you need to know and love yourself. If you do so, you can be authentic, vulnerable, and still be in control of your own power. You will connect the mind with intuition, and that is proven to lead to successful business decisions.

It was only when I truly learned about who I am and what I am capable of (as well as what I am not capable of) that I became a better leader. Moreover, leadership was not difficult anymore because I did not have to pretend to be someone I was not. I showed up as me, with all my perfections and imperfections. That simple act had a tremendous impact on my team. They feel they can be themselves, be vulnerable, and are accepted for who they are.

Besides knowing your values to cultivate self-love, it is also important to continue to:

- *Practice self-compassion*: treat yourself with the same kindness and understanding that you would offer to a good friend. Especially during challenging times, it may be difficult to do this as some of the voices may come up and tell you: 'see, this is what I mean'. Do not ignore your feelings, look at them, and be compassionate. They are there for a reason: what are they trying to tell you? Maybe that you need to be even more compassionate with yourself.

- *Celebrate your achievements*: acknowledge your successes as if they were a friend, and you are supporting them. No matter how small they may seem. Take pride in your accomplishments and recognize your efforts, and don't forget to have fun. Do not take yourself so seriously. Also, things that go wrong can be funny sometimes!

- *Practice gratitude*: once you love yourself for who you truly are, you will notice that happiness is in the smaller things in life. Being grateful for all those small things helps you to cultivate love and compassion.

- *Watch your boundaries:* there may be reminders that you need to reestablish the boundaries you set.

- *Do things that you love* to do make time for things that

give you energy and make you happy (they are part of the self-care too).

- *Surround yourself with people that you love* and want to be with and help you to grow.

- *Seek help when needed.* If you feel you need help, reach out.

Exercise: Survey

Please complete the survey from Chapter 1 about confidence again. When you compare your score with your previous score? What do you see? I believe in you having gained more confidence. And seeing changes occur in your life and business for the better.

Please choose one of the answers for each of the following questions and write down your choice:

1.How confident are you about your physical appearance?
A) Not very confident
B) Moderately confident
C) Very confident

2. How confident do you feel about your abilities to handle challenges at work or in your career?
A) Not very confident
B) Moderately confident
C) Very confident

3. How confident are you in your communication skills, including speaking, listening, and expressing yourself effectively?

    A) Not very confident

    B) Moderately confident

    C) Very confident

4. When it comes to personal relationships, how confident are you in forming and maintaining meaningful connections with others?

    A) Not very confident

    B) Moderately confident

    C) Very confident

5. How confident are you in managing your finances and making sound financial decisions?

    A) Not very confident

    B) Moderately confident

    C) Very confident

6. Regarding your physical health and fitness, how confident are you in your ability to maintain a healthy lifestyle and make positive choices?

    A) Not very confident

    B) Moderately confident

    C) Very confident

7. When faced with adversity or setbacks, how confident are you in your resilience and ability to bounce back?

A) Not very confident

B) Moderately confident

C) Very confident

8. How confident do you feel about setting and achieving personal goals or aspirations?

A) Not very confident

B) Moderately confident

C) Very confident

9. In social situations or group settings, how confident are you in your ability to contribute meaningfully and feel comfortable?

A) Not very confident

B) Moderately confident

C) Very confident

10. When it comes to decision-making, how confident are you in your ability to trust your instincts and make choices that align with your values?

A) Not very confident

B) Moderately confident

C) Very confident

Scoring:

For each answer, assign the following points:

A) 1 point

B) 2 points

C) 3 points

Add up the points from all 10 questions to determine your overall confidence score. The higher the score, the greater the self-perceived confidence in various areas of life.

11 points (Low Confidence): It seems that there are various areas where you have room to grow. The good thing is that when you work on one area to gain more confidence, you will find that in other areas, you automatically gain more confidence too. You are on the right track with this book. Every step forward, no matter how small, is a step towards personal empowerment.

12-21 points (Moderate Confidence): In various aspects of your life, you already possess a solid foundation of confidence. This score indicates that you're already on the path to self-assurance. Look at the areas in your life where you want to gain more confidence and work on those. With each challenge you face and overcome, you'll continue to strengthen your belief in yourself.

22-33 points (High Confidence): Your high confidence score shows a deep sense of self-assurance and resilience. You approach life's opportunities and challenges with unwavering belief in your abilities. Your confidence inspires others and opens doors to limitless possibilities. However, even with high confidence, there's always room for growth and refinement. Embrace each new experience as an opportunity to further strengthen and expand your confidence, empowering yourself to reach even greater heights.

No matter what your scores are, life will always throw some challenges your way that may cause moments in which you feel low self-esteem. The trick is how to bounce back and regain your confidence.

If you feel that others around you can use more confidence too, please tell them about or give them this book. Show compassion with others who do not have a lot of confidence yet, and remember where you came from, too.

Self-love is a journey, not a destination. Be patient with yourself and embrace the process of growth and self-discovery. You deserve to love yourself fully and unconditionally. It is my greatest wish for you to be able to feel self-love and cultivate it and create more of it, as it will change your life and business for the better.

CHAPTER 8

Final Page

Now that you have come to reading one of the last pages of this book, I hope you feel a difference and have more confidence and that it shows at work.

Moving from being insecure to selflove does not happen overnight and life will throw you curveballs that have an impact on your confidence again. But the great thing is, by doing the exercises and by continuing to work on the connection with your heart and gut you will regain your confidence and selflove again. You will increase your resilience and that builds confidence too. Loving is a verb and requires continuous work.

By loving you, as the true self you are not only doing a favour to yourself, but also to others around you. Do not deprive them of the light you are: SHINE.

It does not have to be and go perfect, as long as we accept and love that we are *PERFECTLY IMPERFECT*.

Written with love and the best intentions,

Karina Klaassen

If you wish to continue your journey further, please have a look at my website:

www.confidenceatwork.nl or

www.karinaklaassen.nl

Acknowledgements

Thanks to everyone and everything that led me to write this book, including all those who allowed me to interview them and share their stories.

A special thanks to my husband, Frans for loving me unconditionally, for his unwavering support to write this book and giving me the space to evolve and develop my self-love.

About the Author

Karina Klaassen

As you close this book, you've shared in the transformative journey that led Karina Klaassen from profound insecurity and corporate burnout to becoming an advocate for resilience and self-empowerment. Karina's story continues through her work as the owner of HAPPIBUZZ she helps individuals and organizations reconnect with their essence and thrive.

With over three decades of experience in multinational and multicultural companies, Karina understands the professional challenges many face. Her own burnout was a turning point, leading her to realize that happiness and stress-resilience can be nurtured. This revelation reshaped her life and now aims to inspire yours through this book.

Karina's approach is grounded in both academic knowledge and practical experience. As a certified Happiness and Heartcoherence Coach, facilitator for the Energy Codes, and holder of an MBA in Organisational Happiness, she blends corporate wisdom with holistic well-being practices. Her background in Design adds a creative problem-solving dimension to her methods.

Through HAPPIBUZZ, Karina offers leadership training, organizational happiness consulting, and coaching. Her method goes beyond quick fixes, focusing on reconnecting with one's core self to achieve lasting happiness and resilience—a journey you've begun by reading this book.

Outside of her professional endeavours, Karina finds balance and inspiration in her daily yoga practice, her 30-year marriage, and her dedication to continuous learning and personal development. Once plagued by deep-seated insecurities, she has transformed her life through relentless self-improvement and now empowers others to do the same.

As you reflect on the insights and strategies you've gained, remember that your journey towards greater confidence and self-advocacy is ongoing. Karina invites you to continue this journey:

Visit www.confidenceatwork.nl to learn more about upcoming workshops.

Follow Karina on social media for inspiration and tips.

Share your own story of transformation inspired by this book using #MindYourConfidence.

Thank you for allowing Karina to be a part of your path to empowerment. May you move forward with renewed confidence, ready to advocate for yourself and create the life and career you desire.